*To M.
friend —
Love,
Mary*

SECRET
ORLANDO

A Guide to the Weird, Wonderful, and Obscure

John W. Brown
and Joshua Ginsberg

REEDY PRESS

Reedy Press
PO Box 5131
St. Louis, MO 63139
www.reedypress.com

Library of Congress Control Number: 2023938884
ISBN: 9781681064918

Design by Jill Halpin

Unless otherwise indicated, all photos are courtesy of the authors or in the public domain.

We (the publisher and the author) have done our best to provide the most accurate information available when this book was completed. However, we make no warranty, guarantee, or promise about the accuracy, completeness, or currency of the information provided, and we expressly disclaim all warranties, express or implied. Please note that attractions, company names, addresses, websites, and phone numbers are subject to change or closure, and this is outside of our control. We are not responsible for any loss, damage, injury, or inconvenience that may occur due to the use of this book. When exploring new destinations, please do your homework before you go. You are responsible for your own safety and health when using this book.

Printed in the United States of America
23 24 25 26 27   5 4 3 2 1

This book is dedicated to my FOX 35 coworkers
and the numerous viewers who have piqued my interest
with questions about Orlando mysteries. It's a daily occurrence
that someone mentions a topic that sends me on a mission to find
answers. And it's dedicated to my family and friends who come to
Orlando looking for something more than just the typical tourist
attractions. Finally, I have some answers for you!

—John W. Brown

My portion of this work is dedicated to all those who wander;
to all those many others who embrace, enable, or just accept the
undeniable need for some of us to wander; and to the memory
of my uncle, Hank Litvin.

—Joshua Ginsberg

Disston Sugar Mill Ruins

CONTENTS

ACKNOWLEDGMENTS

BY JOHN W. BROWN

As with any book, a writer can never do it by themself. It takes so many people, places, and experiences to make it truly come to life. So first of all, I want to thank my wife, Teresa, and daughters, Lauren and Sophia, for going to so many of these places with me. In fact, Sophia took many of the pictures contained in this book. Also, thanks to all the people who allowed us to visit your "secret" places to see what makes them so interesting. I can't wait to go back and see them all again. And thanks to my FOX 35 family who gave me so many ideas of places to visit. It truly did take a village, and trips to the Villages, to make this book a reality.

ACKNOWLEDGMENTS

BY JOSHUA GINSBERG

With each book I write, it seems there are more people I want to thank and less space in which to do it. I will provide a more complete list on my blog, terraincognitaamericanus.blogspot.com, but for now I'd like to thank the many individuals and organizations within and beyond Orlando that kindly opened their strange and wondrous worlds to me. Thank you to my coauthor, John, for joining me on this adventure, and to everyone at Reedy Press for putting us together and keeping us on track. I am grateful beyond words to all of the friends and family who patiently listened to me read them the same sentence a dozen times, and above all, my love and gratitude to my wife, Jen, and our intrepid companion Tinker Bell.

INTRODUCTION

BY JOHN W. BROWN

Let's face it, Walt Disney put Orlando on the map when he decided to build his theme park mecca in the area, and he even reminded everyone that "it all started with a mouse." But Mickey Mouse and Walt Disney World are just a part of this amazing story that is Orlando and central Florida, which had its beginning long before Walt flew over the area on November 22, 1963.

In addition to the long history of this area, there are some pretty cool secrets as well. Take, for example, the name Orlando. It's hard to believe, but nobody even knows where the name came from. The area was first named Jernigan when Aaron Jernigan arrived at this barren tropical land in Mosquito County in the 1840s because the government was giving away free land. Once the area was chosen to be the new city of government for Orange County, city leaders changed the name to Orlando, although there is no definitive reason for the name.

So here we are, "Orlando: The City Beautiful." It truly is paradise to many of us who choose to call it home. It's an amazing place with wonderful people and a history that is exceptional, both pre–Disney World (1971) and post–Disney World. And yes, we have uncovered a lot of secrets in making our way around Orlando, the theme parks, and all of central Florida. We are the theme park capital of the world, the biggest tourist destination in the country, one of the fastest-growing cities in America, and we are just getting started. So let's explore some of the secrets of our area to see where we are and where we've come from to understand what makes this place so special.

INTRODUCTION

BY JOSHUA GINSBERG

This is a book about Orlando and the surrounding areas. The Magic Kingdom, Celebration, and the Central Florida Tourism Oversight District (collectively "Walt Disney World") are not Orlando but rather an entirely separate universe. At least, that's what everyone we talked to says. Does mouse and company find its way into this book? Of course it does—it's as unavoidable as traffic on I-4, but for the most part we've tried to keep it to a minimum. That's not to say that there's anything at all wrong with having a great family vacation, mouse ears and all, to one of the best-loved travel destinations on planet Earth, where you can have exactly the sort of curated and manufactured experience you expect. There are also plenty of great guidebooks for that kind of vacation. But this is a different type of travel book, one that mostly begins where the monorail ends.

What awaits you in Orlando that isn't described in travel brochures and hotel rack cards? Natural wonders like the bioluminescent algae you can kayak through at night, unique communities with bizarre backstories like the spiritualist camp Cassadaga, vestiges of lost attractions, strangely specific museums, curio shops, modern ruins, and everywhere phantom traces of Orlando's little-known past intertwining with its perpetual dreams and visions of the future. At that nexus, between what was and what may yet be, anything becomes possible. Suffice it to say, if Florida is the land of reinvention, then Orlando might qualify as its secret capital—visited by millions but really deeply seen and experienced by surprisingly few.

That's where we come in—to help take you off the main roads, back in time and even into space, to less-visited locations, but never so far that you can't easily find your way back again. You might have to plan ahead, or drive or hike a while to find some of these places, but if you're like us, you might agree that the effort it takes to reach some of these places only makes them more enticing. So we invite you to delve deeper into the lost, hidden, and overlooked nooks and crannies of Orlando, that you may discover for yourself the hidden face of the City Beautiful.

One final word of advice: don't mess with gators . . . or with the swans, for that matter.

ORLANDO'S LEGENDARY LITERARY LAUNCHPAD

Where was author Jack Kerouac living when his book _On the Road_ was published?

Separating fact from fiction regarding the life and times of Beat Generation author Jack Kerouac can be every bit as daunting a task as trying to figure out where the punctuation belongs in one of his stream-of-consciousness passages. Nevertheless, in 1996, after extensive research and discussions with Kerouac's brother-in-law, reporter Bob Kealing was able to locate the cottage where the author and his mother had rented two rooms between July 1957 and the spring of 1958. During that time, _On the Road_ was published and the follow-up novel, _The Dharma Bums_, was written.

When Kealing finally stood before the 1920s cottage, he might have been a little crestfallen. It was still standing but badly run down, not unlike Kerouac himself coming off one of his many Benzedrine-fueled cross-country road trips. When Kealing's piece came out in the _Orlando Sentinel_, he found kindred spirits in local bookstore owners Marty and Jan Cummins, who proposed that they set up a nonprofit to acquire and transform the cottage into a retreat for up-and-coming writers.

Thus was born the Kerouac Project of Orlando and with the help of like-minded benefactors, the cottage has now provided three-month rent-free residencies for more than 65 writers. It has also received visits from many Beat Generation luminaries

THE FORMER HOME OF JACK KEROUAC

WHAT: The cottage where Jack Kerouac lived when he first became a published author

WHERE: 1418 Clouser Ave.

COST: Free to take a picture out front

PRO TIP: Visitors are not typically allowed inside, unless there is a special event.

Exterior of the Kerouac House, which continues to serve as a residence for writers.
Photo by Joshua Ginsberg

including poet, publisher, and City Lights Books owner Lawrence Ferlinghetti; musician Steve Allen; Carolyn Cassady (widow of Kerouac's frequent partner in crime, Neal); and others. Funds from grants and renting out the adjoining house ensure that Kerouac's legacy will continue by enabling a new generation of writers to start their own creative endeavors, without ever missing a beat.

If you feel so inspired, you could take a thematically appropriate road trip to see the last place the author lived and the bar he frequented in St. Petersburg. Consult *Secret Tampa Bay* for details.

THE HIDDEN HIGHWAY TO FLORIDA

Where is the original highway to Florida still hidden in plain sight?

One of the original brick roadways connecting old Florida to the rest of the country still exists in some places. In fact, you may have walked the historic brick road and not even known that you were experiencing a bit of Florida transportation history. It was called the Old Dixie Highway, and this was the road that early cars drove on to get to Florida. However, the combination of skinny tires and sandy brick roads proved to be a tough combination for travelers. Thankfully, as more modern highways moved to other parcels of land, elements of the now "secret" road were left behind.

The Old Dixie Highway in Florida opened in 1925 and ran from Michigan all the way down to south Florida, right through central Florida. This primitive roadway helped connect this growing region to people from up north who were looking to experience the Sunshine State. Although it was one highway, there were two routes through Florida. One ran along the coast near where US 1 now lies. The other came through Gainesville, Ocala, Orlando, Kissimmee, and then toward Bartow. Just north of Orlando, the approximately seven-foot-wide brick road ran alongside Lake Lily in Maitland where a portion of it still exists. This portion was actually built in 1915 as the first "paved" road in Florida and later incorporated into the highway.

The idea for the Old Dixie Highway came from Carl Fisher, a developer in Miami Beach. He knew that if a good road was built from north to south, his town would eventually attract more tourists.

The Old Dixie Highway from Michigan with two primary routes through Florida. Portions of the road still exist throughout the state.

Farther north, there is a 10-mile stretch that history buffs still make road trips to see. The Old Brick Road, as it's called, looks more like a sandy road through the marshlands of Florida as it cuts between Espanola in Flagler County and Hastings in St. Johns County. This stretch of history was added to the National Register of Historic Places back in 2005.

THE OLD DIXIE HIGHWAY

WHAT: The original brick road to Florida

WHERE: Numerous places

Visible in Lake Lily Park, 701 Lake Lily Dr., Maitland

The 10-mile stretch can be accessed near 3130 N Old Dixie Hwy., Espanola

COST: Free

PRO TIP: In Maitland, bring your walking shoes as the old highway is incorporated into a walking trail around a beautiful lake.

ANCIENT REPTILE VISIT

Can you really get into Gatorland at night and feed the alligators?

If you spend any amount of time in Florida, you are bound to see an alligator. No matter how many times you see them, you likely still look at them with a sense of awe. The only thing cooler might be seeing them at night when their eyes light up the darkness, which is exactly what you get to do during the Gator Night Shine trip.

Gatorland truly is one of the original roadside attractions in Florida, dating back to 1949. That little attraction with a handful of alligators has now grown into a massive operation with hundreds of alligators spread out across the very "Florida" themed park. There are also exotic birds and some of the biggest snakes on the planet. They even have a zip-line tour that whizzes you right over the heads of the giant reptiles.

But this theme park has also become a major player in alligator education and conservation. Since the park was established in 1949, the mission of the park grew from just housing a massive collection of alligators to letting others know more about the special creatures. The park even established the Gatorland Global conservation program, which is designed to protect, conserve, and educate people about American alligators and their close relatives and the environments in which they live.

Now to the spooky nighttime experience. Once the sun goes down, you and up to 25 friends can grab some flashlights, a little gator food, and prowl around the park (with a guide, of course!).

GATORLAND

WHAT: Gator Night Shine

WHERE: 14501 S Orange Blossom Trail

COST: Gator Night Shine is $24.99. Regular admission to the park is $32.99 for adults and $22.99 for children.

PRO TIP: Do the Screamin' Gator zip line! On your zips, you fly across 130 alligators in the Breeding Marsh for an experience you will never forget.

More than 2,000 alligators call Gatorland home, but so do hundreds of other species of animals. Photo by Sophia Brown

When you shine the lights across the water, the eyes begin to glow from hundreds of these ancient reptiles as they come closer because you also get to feed them. So, if you want to see wild Florida up close and personal, the nighttime is the right time.

Alligators were put on the endangered species list in 1967. Now there are an estimated 1.3 million of these ancient reptiles living in Florida alone.

IF YOU BUILD IT, THEY WILL COME

Where can you step back in time and onto the pitcher's mound of Orlando's first baseball stadium?

In 1914, while Chicago was erecting Wrigley Field, Orlando was constructing a baseball field of its own. Within a decade it had completed a new, all-wooden baseball stadium dedicated as Tinker Field in April of 1923 (named for Hall of Famer Joe Tinker, not for Peter Pan's diminutive sidekick). It featured a field of Georgia clay ringed by a Bermuda sod outfield, with seating for 1,500 fans (larger, it's believed, than Yankee Stadium). From 1923 until 1990, it served as the spring training home for the Cincinnati Reds, the Brooklyn Dodgers, and finally the Washington Senators/Minnesota Twins. Legendary players who trained there include Babe Ruth, Jackie Robinson, Rod Carew, Lou Gehrig, Hank Aaron, and Michael Jordan.

In 1963 the field was rebuilt with 1,000 seats incorporated from Washington DC's Griffith Stadium. The following year, Tinker Field made history unrelated to baseball, when from the pitcher's mound Dr. Martin Luther King Jr. delivered his only public speech in central Florida, known as the "Integration Now" speech.

With the commencement of the reconstruction of the Orlando Citrus Bowl (now Camping World Stadium) in January of 2014, it was announced that the grandstands and other

Built as a WPA project in 1936, Camping World Stadium has changed its name more than a few times. Former names include Orlando Stadium, Tangerine Bowl, Citrus Bowl, Florida Citrus Bowl, and Orlando Citrus Bowl.

The history of Tinker Field is remembered in markers and historical displays. Photo by Joshua Ginsberg

ORLANDO'S FIELD OF DREAMS

WHAT: Tinker Field History Plaza

WHERE: 287 S Tampa Ave.

COST: Free

PRO TIP: Joe Tinker is also remembered elsewhere around the city, including in a plaque outside the building he constructed in 1925 that once housed his real estate offices. It is located at 16 and 18 West Pine St.

buildings in the adjacent Tinker Field would be removed. Given the site's historic significance (to civil rights as well as to minor and major league baseball), the field and diamond were designated an Orlando Historic Landmark in 2015.

Today, outside the front gates, visitors can walk the bases in a miniature replica of the field, read an information display, and sit back in some of the seats from the old stadium. You might still hear music there too, though it probably won't be from an organ—the former field has found new life as an outdoor concert and event venue.

OF CROCS AND CRACKERS

Who is that man in the statue riding a gator in front of the Orange County Regional History Center?

Even in a state packed with colorful historical characters, the Florida cracker cowboys stand out as being an especially memorable bunch. The most famous of these was likely the wisecracking Bone Mizell, who was the subject of a not particularly flattering Frederic Remington painting. His antics, misadventures, and tall tales have become a staple of Florida folklore, but he wasn't the only such notable cowboy. Orlando had its own share of them, including Bunk Baxter, who is said to have supplemented his income with a side hustle as a gator wrestler. He would head into town on market days with a gator

CROCODILE RIDER

WHAT: *Bunk Baxter* sculpture

WHERE: Heritage Square Park, 65 E Central Blvd.

COST: Free to check out the sculptures in the park; museum general admission is $8.

PRO TIP: Don't try riding gators at home, or anywhere for that matter, unless you're a trained professional.

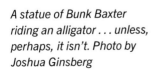

A statue of Bunk Baxter riding an alligator . . . unless, perhaps, it isn't. Photo by Joshua Ginsberg

in tow and, for a small fee, provide a photo opportunity wrestling and sitting atop the reptile with his hands around its jaws. One of these photos, taken by Stanley J. Morrow around 1885, has become one of the most iconic images of Orlando's early days.

Sculptor Scott Shaffer created the life-size bronze statue, titled *Bunk Baxter*, which was placed in Heritage Square Park prior to the museum's opening in 2000. But is it really Bunk Baxter in the photo? Some have argued that it may actually be another early pioneer named John Burl "Bud" Yates II. Also, is that an alligator that he's riding? In the photo, that long, narrow snout sure looks more like that of a crocodile.

Visitors can learn more about the sculpture inside the museum, which contains a great many more curious historical facts. For one thing, prior to becoming a museum, the neoclassical building was a courthouse where the notorious serial killer Ted Bundy was tried. It was also the site of a shooting on January 10, 1984, when Thomas Provenzano killed a bailiff and wounded two others, which served as a catalyst for installing metal detectors in courthouses nationwide.

Cracker cowboy Bone Mizell also has a connection to Orlando. His family was involved in the Barber–Mizell family feud of 1870, and some of his relatives remain there in the small Mizell family cemetery inside of Leu Gardens.

TOMBS OF THE WELL-KNOWN

Why are most of the Orlando city founders buried in one place?

One of the most beautiful and historic places in the entire city of Orlando lies on a hill just south of downtown, yet many people don't know the place exists. The Greenwood Cemetery is where the "who's who" of Orlando are buried. In fact, many of the names on streets and buildings across the city are spending their afterlife together in one perfectly manicured resting place. The 128-acre city-owned cemetery offers a four-mile stroll where you can see the tombstones that made Orlando what it is today. We are talking about names like Beacham, Bumby, Carr, Lee, Parramore, Robinson, and Tinker. Many of them made news headlines during their lives and continued making news after their deaths.

The cemetery was established in 1880, five years after the city of Orlando was incorporated. Eight city founders pooled their money to purchase 26 acres of land to make sure residents had a permanent burial location and called it Orlando Cemetery, later changed to Greenwood.

Greenwood is the only cemetery within the city limits of Orlando that still has burials. It also has the highest point in the city, which is where former Orange County surveyor Samuel Robinson is buried.

The site of the cemetery was chosen due to its location, but that wasn't necessarily a good thing. The area around the urban oasis was once a sinkhole connected by a series of ditches that collected the town's sewage. The area eventually became less of a "toilet" after sewage lines were installed around the city.

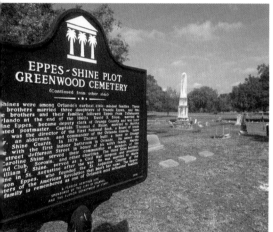

GREENWOOD CEMETERY

WHAT: The burial site of Orlando's founders and city leaders

WHERE: 1603 Greenwood St.

COST: Free

PRO TIP: When the moon is full, the cemetery offers guided Moonlight Walking Tours. The four-mile walking tour showcases about 100 notable grave sites from Orlando history. Sign up quickly because space is limited.

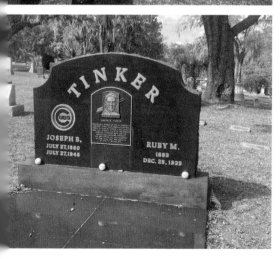

The famous names on headstones around Greenwood Cemetery. Photo by Sophia Brown

A CITY BY ANY OTHER NAME

Why is there no record of the man for whom the city is supposedly named?

Lake Eola could be considered the city's aqueous heart, pumping water rather than blood from its Centennial Fountain. The path around the lake connects monuments, such as the pagoda-like red Chinese Ting, to artworks, an amphitheater, and other features. But one of the monuments there commemorates something that might not have ever really happened.

In 1939, Cherokee Junior High School students placed a marker in honor of Orlando Reeves, for whom the city is allegedly named. According to the plaque, Reeves was killed by Native Americans in the area in September of 1835, around the Second Seminole War. This apocryphal story has dozens of variations, the core of which is that while keeping watch one night, Reeves spotted Seminoles preparing to attack, sounded the warning, and perished in the ensuing conflict, giving his life to save his fellow soldiers.

It's an inspiring story, but there's one tiny problem. No record exists of any Orlando Reeves serving in the area. There was a cattle rancher, Orlando J. Rees (nicknamed "Colonel" Rees), who lived near Fort Gatlin in the 1830s and had documented conflicts with local Seminoles, but Rees had vanished from the historical record by the 1840 census. Is he the basis for the

HOW ORLANDO DIDN'T GET ITS NAME

WHAT: Orlando Reeves Monument

WHERE: Lake Eola Park, on the eastern edge of the lake path near the western terminus of E Washington St.

COST: Free

PRO TIP: If you're keeping track of your steps, the path around the lake is exactly 0.9 miles long.

The marker by the path around Lake Eola tells just one of the stories behind how the city got its name.
Photo by Joshua Ginsberg

Orlando Reeves story? Or was it a different "Mr. Orlando" who died nearby while taking an ox caravan to Tampa and was buried under a tree with the message, "Here lies Orlando"? Or was it that judge J. G. Speer, who helped organize Orange County in 1856, just happened to like Shakespeare? That would explain both the name of the city and the main street, Rosalind.

So which version, if any, is true? We'll probably never know, but in a city synonymous with manufacturing fantasy and illusion, perhaps a better question is, which version would you like to be true?

There's another statue around Lake Eola that might be more than it appears. *Fantasy Swan* is connected to a book by Angi Perretti about a girl named "AngiArts" and her feathered companion as they go time traveling in search of inspiration.

MURDER MOST FOWL

How did a gaggle of quarrelsome swans become a symbol of Orlando?

While you're checking out the unusual monuments and artworks around Lake Eola, you'll likely encounter some of the city's most famous residents—the many large swans that have no compunction about letting visitors know that the lake belongs to them. Apparently, their mean streak isn't something new but rather a trait inherited from their original progenitor.

The story begins in 1910, when English merchant Charles Lord settled near Lake Lucerne and later introduced two pairs of swans, Billy Bluebeard and Sally Swan and another short-lived couple. More swans were brought in, but, as the people of Orlando soon learned, the birds can be notoriously and violently territorial.

Though it's unlikely that the swans had any royal connections, as Lord and the *Orlando Sentinel* sometimes claimed (more likely Lord bought them in Connecticut), Billy took to the role of royal pain, behaving every bit as badly as any English tyrant, regularly assaulting and chasing visitors. As if to legitimize their faux British background, Billy and Sally's romance played out like an avian version of Sid and Nancy when Billy flew into a rage and murdered his mate for taking a swim without him.

Billy took a new mate, Mary, but she left him for a younger swan named Charlie, against whom Billy was no match. His continued attacks got him exiled to another lake where it is said that he passed away at the age of 78. Following his demise in 1933, Billy was stuffed and placed in the foyer of the appropriately named

---

While the noble lineage of Lake Eola's swans is dubious at best, nearby Lakeland's swans are the real deal—they were a gift to the city from Queen Elizabeth II in 1957.

Seen here, a new generation of swans will one day carry on Billy's contentious legacy. Photo by Joshua Ginsberg

dry goods store W. H. Swan & Co. Eventually he migrated to the Orange County Regional History Center, where he has resided ever since.

Though Billy's reign of terror may have ended, he lives on around Like Eola in murals, swan-shaped boats, and countless ill-tempered offspring.

WHAT: The swans of Lake Eola and the preserved body of Billy Bluebeard

WHERE: Billy Bluebeard is at the Orlando County Regional History Center located at Heritage Square Park, 65 E Central Blvd.

COST: Free to check out the sculptures in the park; museum general admission is $8.

PRO TIP: If you want to feed the swans, you can use lettuce, spinach, or the pellet food found at the parks.

AN ESCAPE UNDER ORANGE AVENUE

Did celebrities really escape from crowds using a downtown tunnel?

In a city with the amazing history of Orlando, you know there must be plenty of secrets. But there are some stories that seem to captivate locals and guests alike, especially the story about the hidden tunnel connecting the historic Beacham Theatre and the Angebilt Hotel where the rich and famous stayed while in Orlando.

Let's get the backstory first to fully understand why a hidden passageway would be necessary. The Angebilt Hotel was Florida luxury at its finest. The 11-story building was the place to stay in the early 1900s . . . if you had the means to do so. Names like Thomas Edison, Henry Ford, Joan Crawford, and Harvey Firestone all stayed there. Meanwhile, the Beacham Theatre across Orange Avenue was where vaudeville stars would come to perform.

So here is where the legend lies. The fact is, there is a tunnel that was connected to a trapdoor behind the stage at the old theater. That tunnel did go under Orange Avenue to the Angebilt, which still stands today under a different name, but with the historic A's still adorning the structure. The problem is the tunnel appears to be too narrow to traverse in many places. Sure, the rich and famous could

DOWNTOWN ORLANDO HISTORIC WALKING TOUR

WHAT: A trip around the city to see our historical secrets

WHERE: 511 W South St. is where the tour begins at the Wells'Built Hotel.

COST: Free

PRO TIP: It's best to do the walking tour on a weekend morning when it's nice and quiet. The tour is less than three miles but has a lot of history packed inside a short area.

Angebilt, now and then. The historic hotel still stands along Orange Avenue. Photo by Sophia Brown

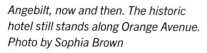

have crawled, but getting them to take such drastic action may have been a bit of a stretch. A local publicist says it's much more likely that the stars' handlers made a distraction allowing the A-listers to walk across the street unseen. Some historians also speculate that the tunnel may have been a place to hide liquor during Prohibition.

The Beacham is recognized as being one of the original venues where electronic dance music originated in the 1990s. This helped usher in the popularity of "raves," which trace their roots to downtown Orlando.

SWIMMING IN SECRETS

What makes Dr. Lucky Meisenheimer's home one of the most visited private residences in Florida?

Those familiar with Dr. Lucky Meisenheimer professionally know him as a well-respected and sought-after dermatological surgeon, but that accounts for just a fraction of those who've met him.

The bulk of visitors to his home, which is one of the most visited private residences statewide, are there for Lucky's Lake Swims, which began in 1989 in the lake behind his house. The swims occur at 6:30 a.m. Monday through Friday, open to anyone who can arrive on time and comfortably swim a kilometer. The swims are, according to Meisenheimer, "one of the last free activities in Orlando." Participants are invited to sign their names to his patio ceiling (having run out of space on his back wall).

Just on the other side of those autographed walls, and unbeknown to most affixing their names, is another reason why some know Doc Lucky—for his role as chairman of the National Yo-Yo Hall of Fame and his title as owner of the world's largest collection of yo-yos. The collection includes now likely north of 10,000 yo-yos and is valued at over a quarter of a million dollars. Unlike the lake swim, which is open to the public, the best way to see his private yo-yo collection is via his web show, *Doc Lucky's Yo-Yo Talk*, or by making an appointment.

Both open-water swimmers and yo-yo aficionados likely fail to realize yet one more reason that some know the doctor is for what lurks deeper in his home: his collection of zombie memorabilia

---

Doc Lucky isn't the only curious collector in town. Orlando resident Becky Marts has collected and cataloged more than 21,000 banana labels from all over the world.

Doc Lucky hosting one of his lake swims (top) and peering out from a curtain of yo-yos (bottom). Photos by Jacquie Meisenheimer

YO-YOS, ZOMBIES, AND LAKE SWIMMERS

WHAT: Doc Lucky's home and lake swims

WHERE: 6645 Lake Cane Dr.

COST: Free

PRO TIP: If you plan to attend one of the lake swims, consider completing the waiver at luckyslakeswim.com ahead of time.

and movie props (he is, after all, the author of *The Zombie Cause Dictionary*).

So what does Doc Lucky do with all his spare time? Well, for that he has underwater hockey (he plays for the defending state champions), but that, of course, is a whole other thing.

THE CITY HAUNTINGLY BEAUTIFUL

Does downtown Orlando get any visitors . . . from beyond the grave?

Before it became "The City Beautiful," Orlando was "The Phenomenal City," and given all of the unexplained phenomena found there today, perhaps that first moniker was more apt. Probably no one is more knowledgeable about local spirits than Ting Rappa, who has been communicating with them since she was a child. She has turned that unusual gift into a career as the founder of American Ghost Adventures.

With so many haunts to choose from, routes vary from tour to tour, but some you might visit include:

- Greenwood Cemetery: With 100 acres, it's not surprising that at least a few of those who call this their final resting place aren't always at rest. Confederate soldiers are said to roam near the oak trees, and children have been heard playing, laughing, and crying in the section known as Babyland 3.

- The Kress Building: Now home to Kres Chophouse, in its former life this art deco building was a department store, and according to numerous witnesses, some of those shoppers are still milling about. Everything from strange noises and footfalls to full-bodied apparitions are on the menu here, making it a veritable paranormal smorgasbord. Bon appétit!

- The Rogers Building: Orlando's oldest building is currently managed by the Downtown Arts District, but some of its former guests and tenants, it seems, aren't quite ready to leave. Foremost among them is the wife of Gordon Rogers, sometimes seen on the stairway or wandering the halls.

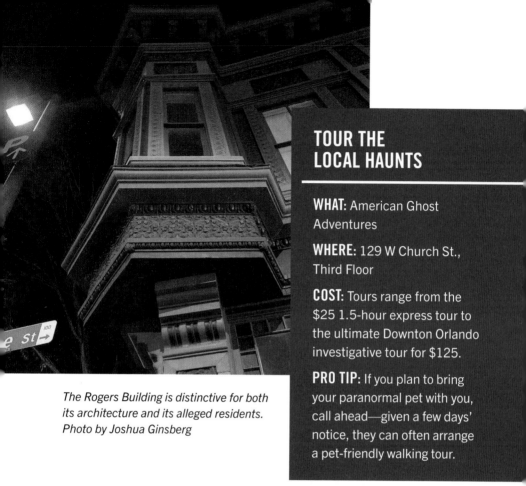

The Rogers Building is distinctive for both its architecture and its alleged residents. Photo by Joshua Ginsberg

TOUR THE LOCAL HAUNTS

WHAT: American Ghost Adventures

WHERE: 129 W Church St., Third Floor

COST: Tours range from the $25 1.5-hour express tour to the ultimate Downton Orlando investigative tour for $125.

PRO TIP: If you plan to bring your paranormal pet with you, call ahead—given a few days' notice, they can often arrange a pet-friendly walking tour.

Other popular spots with the postmortem crowd include the Orange County Regional History Center, the Super 8 motel on International Drive, and many others, but we don't want to give too much away. Better to let Rappa and her experienced team part the veil and guide you deeper into the city's dark heart.

Another ghost hunting "hot spot" can be found just north of Orlando: the treacherous patch of highway known as the I-4 Dead Zone. Drive carefully.

BUILT TO LAST

During the era of segregation, where could Black visitors to Orlando find a place to stay?

Entrepreneurs are those rare individuals possessed of both vision and business savvy, who see opportunity where others see only challenges. The category includes the entertainment mogul Walt Disney, dealmakers like Hamilton Disston, inventors such as Aaron Fechter, and one Dr. William Monroe Wells.

Dr. Wells arrived in Orlando in 1917 as the second African American physician in central Florida. He set up his practice in the Parramore neighborhood, treating the sick, delivering babies, and providing for African Americans all of the medical care that most White doctors did not. He soon realized that it wasn't just health services the community lacked—it also had no hotels or entertainment for Black residents and visitors. He took to the challenge of addressing those gaps.

Despite the difficulty of securing loans and financing, by 1925 he had finished building the Wells'Built Hotel, which gave the neighborhood an economic boost, featuring hotel rooms on the second floor and retail space on the first floor. Ella Fitzgerald, Thurgood Marshall, Jackie Robinson, Ray Charles, Cab Calloway, and B. B. King are just some of hotel's more notable guests.

Having given Black travelers a place to stay when they visited, Dr. Wells turned his focus to giving those travelers a reason to visit. Thus he created the South Street Casino as a gathering

---

The Wells'Built Hotel was listed in *The Negro Motorist Green Book* as one of the places where Black travelers could find accommodations. In the 1956 edition of the book, it was one of only two such hotels in Orlando (the other was the Sun-Glo Motel).

The unassuming exterior of the Wells'Built Museum belies the trove of cultural treasures within. Photos by Joshua Ginsberg

place and venue for many of the Black musicians and performers along what was known as the Chitlin' Circuit.

Although Dr. Wells passed away in 1957, his vision lives on. The Wells'Built Hotel was added to the National Register of Historic Places in 2000 and reopened the following year as the Wells'Built Museum of African American History and Culture. Today it displays memorabilia and information about Orlando's Black history as well as a re-creation of one of the hotel rooms with authentic 1930s furnishings.

PRESCRIPTION FOR SUCCESS

WHAT: The Wells'Built Museum of African American History and Culture

WHERE: 511 W South St.

COST: $5 for adults, $3 for students and seniors, $2 for children ages 4–13

PRO TIP: You can get a combination ticket for both the Wells'Built Museum and the Orange County Regional History Center for $10.

ROCKIN' IN THE FREE WORLD

What is a relic of the Cold War doing behind a Hard Rock Cafe?

For 28 years, from 1961 to 1989, the stark gray concrete Berlin Wall split communist East Germany from noncommunist West Germany and came to symbolize a divide that was as much ideological as physical. Some 5,000 individuals successfully escaped from East to West Germany, and about the same number were captured by East German authorities. Another 191 were killed while attempting to flee. On November 9, 1989, while the world watched, the wall came down, and pieces of it almost immediately began to circulate around the globe.

Today, the Hard Rock Cafe in Orlando's City Walk represents an empire built on the western ideas of rock and roll, entertainment, and capitalism—seemingly about as distant from remnants of Cold War enmity as one could get. Yet there, behind the restaurant, in what is perhaps the very last place on earth you would expect to find it, is a fully intact four-meter-tall portion of the wall. A plaque at the base provides a short synopsis of the wall and its enduring significance as a "piece of history that symbolizes the fall of oppression."

For those seeking to delve deeper into the restaurant's rock-and-roll reliquary, the opportunity to do so is often available for those who know to ask. Inquire with the reservationist about the

BEHIND THE MUSIC

WHAT: Section of the Berlin Wall behind the Hard Rock Cafe

WHERE: 6050 Universal Blvd.

COST: Free to walk behind the restaurant to see the slab of the Berlin Wall. The VIP tour is for paying customers.

PRO TIP: The best time to catch the VIP tour is on a weekday before happy hour.

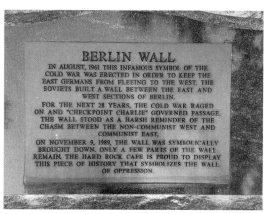

BERLIN WALL

IN AUGUST, 1961 THIS INFAMOUS SYMBOL OF THE
COLD WAR WAS ERECTED IN ORDER TO KEEP THE
EAST GERMANS FROM FLEEING TO THE WEST. THE
SOVIETS BUILT A WALL BETWEEN THE EAST AND
WEST SECTIONS OF BERLIN.
FOR THE NEXT 28 YEARS, THE COLD WAR RAGED
ON AND "CHECKPOINT CHARLIE" GOVERNED PASSAGE.
THE WALL STOOD AS A HARSH REMINDER OF THE
CHASM BETWEEN THE NON-COMMUNIST WEST AND
COMMUNIST EAST.
ON NOVEMBER 9, 1989, THE WALL WAS SYMBOLICALLY
BROUGHT DOWN. ONLY A FEW PARTS OF THE WALL
REMAIN. THE HARD ROCK CAFE IS PROUD TO DISPLAY
THIS PIECE OF HISTORY THAT SYMBOLIZES THE WALL
OF OPPRESSION.

This large, preserved portion of the Berlin Wall is hiding in plain sight around the back of the Hard Rock Cafe. Photo by Joshua Ginsberg

VIP tour, which lasts about 45 minutes and takes visitors behind the scenes, through the Woodstock Room, the John Lennon Room, and into the Attic. Along the way you'll see a wall of bricks from the Cavern Club where the Beatles played hundreds of concerts, the actual Voice-O-Graph booth where Elvis Presley recorded his first song (for a whopping 35 cents), and a great deal more.

Tucked away in Hyland Oaks Estates is another unusual rock monument—a replica of Elvis Presley's Graceland. Be respectful if you stop for a photo—it's not open to the public.

THE UNBELIEVABLY TRUE STORAGE

Where do Ripley's trove of treasures reside when they're not on display?

Remember that warehouse from the Indiana Jones movies, filled with crates of legendary relics and artifacts? It turns out that such a place does actually exist, and it is intentionally tucked away deep within the most inconspicuous office building you've never noticed.

It's common knowledge that Ripley Entertainment is a veritable empire of strangeness as the largest operator of walk-through tourist attractions on planet Earth. Lesser known is the fact that Orlando is the company's global headquarters, and known to all but a handful is that their corporate offices house their publishing branch, the studio where their wax museum figures are created, and yes, a warehouse packed with curiosities that either are not or cannot be displayed.

Beyond the reception area (and the preserved flap of woolly mammoth hide) is the production area, where on any given day artists may be designing, sculpting, assembling, and dressing historical figures, pop stars, or tech billionaires like Elon Musk.

Adjacent to the creative workspace is the warehouse, stacked floor to ceiling with crates (marked with things like "world's longest human fingernails"), automobile-shaped coffins, the famous dress worn by both Marilyn Monroe and Kim Kardashian, Berlin Wall fragments, robots, Olympic torches,

Robert Ripley became the first person to broadcast underwater from Marineland in St. Augustine, Florida, on February 23, 1940. Can you believe it?

The world's largest ball of human hair is just one of the fascinating things you might find at Ripley's Entertainment warehouse. Photo by Joshua Ginsberg

WHERE HOUSE?

WHAT: Ripley's Entertainment offices and warehouse

WHERE: Warehouse location: redacted; Odditorium location: 8201 International Dr.

COST: Ripley's Odditorium is $18.99 for children 3—11 and $27.99 for adults (plus $3 for a souvenir collection book).

PRO TIP: There is another way to visit the warehouse: just make and donate to them some *Guinness Book* record-setting oddity, like a functioning spacecraft made out of gummy bears. Easy, right?

statues of Egyptian deities made from junk metal, and oh so much human hair.

Before you drop by though, assuming you could locate it, you should know that it is not open to the public (well, not without a reason at least as good as writing a book about the weirdness of Orlando). You can, however, have more fun trying your hand at managing the warehouses' inventory through an interactive display at the Ripley's Odditorium in Orlando.

Rest assured though, whatever is in that warehouse, they have top people working on it right now.

OLD RECORDS NEVER DIE

Where do audiophiles and rock-and-roll legends shop for music when they're in Orlando?

Rock and Roll Heaven, owned by brothers Ray and Freddy Ehmen since 1986, is something of a musical time capsule packed with rare recordings, vintage memorabilia, and a whole lotta love. And, of course, enough tales to fill a season of *Behind the Music*—like how they became the first store to carry demos from a local band that went on to make heavy metal history, or the day Judas Priest lead singer Rob Halford stopped in for directions to a bar, or the time that Lou Pearlman dropped by to introduce the members of a new band he'd assembled locally, called the Backstreet Boys.

Nothing though lives on in the annals of local music history quite like the true story of how the King of Pop once made an offer that the store refused. Freddy was behind the counter one day in the late 1980s when several security guards filtered into the store. Freddy didn't pay much attention until he heard an unmistakably high-pitched voice. He knew who it was, even before he turned to see Michael Jackson wearing his iconic letterman's jacket from the "Thriller" video. Jackson made his way around the store but fixated on a marionette of Moe from the Three Stooges and asked if it was for sale. Freddy responded that he couldn't sell it without consulting his brother, who owned it. Jackson increased his offer. Freddy tried and failed to contact Ray. Jackson again upped the ante, producing six crisp hundred-dollar bills from a briefcase full of them. Ultimately, in what anyone with siblings will

Visitors can still pay homage to the King of Pop and other rock and roll royalty at the store today. Photo by Joshua Ginsberg

agree is the most extraordinary part of the story, Freddy declined to sell his brother's toys. Jackson was understanding about the matter and returned when he was in town next, delaying his private jet's departure for the simple joy of record shopping.

Gone but not forgotten: the country-and-western club Rainbow Ranch opened in 1960 in a red barn along General Hutchison Parkway. It was here that the Five Owls (originally the Whoot Owls) hosted a daily radio show on WHOO. As of 2021, you can once again see the venue's old painted signage.

RISING FROM THE ASHES

How do I find the speakeasy hidden in one of the oldest buildings in downtown Orlando?

If you were to drive by 30 S Magnolia Ave. in downtown Orlando, you would never know there is a magnificent bar hidden inside the historic three-story brick building. You still may not know that bar exists just feet away . . . if you were to get approval to get into the elevator and ride up to the third floor. That is the point of a speakeasy, and when you finally find the right bookshelf to slide open in the secret library, that's when you finally find Mathers Social Gathering.

Mathers Social is located in the Phoenix Building and is perhaps one of the best-kept secrets in downtown Orlando. The building itself brings along a certain mystique and history that most are unaware of. The building was built in the 1870s and was one of Orlando's first brick buildings. The Great Orlando Fire of 1884 gutted this building, but locals decided to spare the structure instead of tearing it down, which is when it took on the name Phoenix. It even became the home of the city's first post office.

For decades it was home to the Mathers Furniture store and other businesses then stayed vacant until 1980 when new owners brought it back to life again. Now, the 1800s-inspired speakeasy takes you back in time as no detail has been overlooked inside

---

The Phoenix may be one of the oldest buildings still standing in Orlando, but the Rogers Building a half block away is the oldest building in downtown. It was built around 1886 and is now home to the Downtown Arts District.

MATHERS SOCIAL GATHERING

WHAT: Speakeasy hidden in one of the oldest buildings in Orlando

WHERE: 30 S Magnolia Ave.

COST: No cost to enter, but must be 21 and a dress code is enforced

PRO TIP: Get there early in the evening if you want to take in the history on the walls before you enjoy food and drinks.

Inside Mathers Social Gathering, a bar hidden in plain sight on Magnolia Avenue. Photo by Sophia Brown

the massive room. Even the drinks have names that transport you to another time like Bathtub Gin and Prohibition Milk & Cookies. But, you have to find the secret door first!

A NIGHT TO REMEMBER

Are you ready to go back . . . to *Titanic*?

Maybe it's you, or your grandmother, or your significant other's coworker's second cousin—whoever it is, you can safely bet that someone in your orbit loves the *Titanic*. Maybe to the point of obsession. For such individuals there is a museum and dinner experience that will beckon to them from the pages of history and from the dark, briny depths of the Atlantic Ocean.

Welcome to Titanic: The Artifact Exhibition, one of two museums owned and operated by EM Group, the only private company with the rights and capabilities to retrieve and display RMS *Titanic* (RMST) objects from the bottom of the sea.

The Orlando museum (the other is in Las Vegas) showcases more than 300 objects that were either actually on the ship when it went down (indicated by the White Star Line logo) or are reproductions. These include everything from dinnerware and luggage to musical instruments, jewelry, and pieces of the ship itself. Upon entering, guests are given a "boarding pass" with the biographical information of one of the passengers. Hold on to that ticket, and at the end you get to scan it and learn the fate of that particular individual.

The museum leads visitors chronologically through a series of rooms designed to replicate walking through the shipyard and port, through the common areas and dining halls, down into the boiler room, and past re-creations of some of the 840 private rooms ranging from the most luxurious to bare-bones

DINNER IN THE DRINK

WHAT: The Artifact Exhibition and First-Class Dinner Gala

WHERE: 7324 International Dr.

COST: Tickets for the museum start at $16.95 for Florida residents; the full dinner experience is $69 per adult and $42 for children ages 7–11.

PRO TIP: The museum can be a little chilly (there is, after all, a manmade iceberg in there); consider bringing along an extra layer.

The combination of authentic artifacts and artistic reproductions makes the museum a one-of-a-kind experience. Photos by Joshua Ginsberg

accommodations for many who were making their way to a new land and life.

There are stops throughout where you can take pictures in front of the iconic Grand Staircase and other locations you might recognize. You can also savor one bittersweet final meal in the company of actors playing Molly Brown, Captain Edward John Smith, and other memorable characters.

If you want a deeper dive into the ocean and its inhabitants, SEA LIFE Orlando Aquarium offers the only 360-degree ocean tunnel in Florida. They also offer behind-the-scenes tours—visit their website for details.

DUST TRACKS ON THE ROAD TO EATONVILLE

What small community played an outsized role in the Harlem Renaissance?

Just miles from downtown Orlando, Eatonville was incorporated in 1887 as the first all-Black self-governed town in the US. While this is certainly enough to earn it a place in the history books, much of its enduring fame is due to one of its uniquely gifted residents who went on to become a world-renowned, trailblazing author and folklorist.

Technically, Zora Neale Hurston was born in Notasulga, Alabama, on January 7, 1891, but the following year her family moved to Eatonville. There she grew up in a town with a "Black charter, Black mayor, Black town council, Black marshal and all" (*Dust Tracks on a Road*). Eatonville lodged deep in her psyche, even when she left for Baltimore, Maryland, in 1917, then Howard University (where the literary magazine, *Stylus*, published her first story), then to Barnard College and Harlem, where she became a central figure in the Harlem Renaissance.

Despite having penned *Their Eyes Were Watching God, Tell My Horse, Dust Tracks on a Road*, and other works, by 1950 she returned to Florida nearly penniless and still virtually unknown. Following a short stint covering the Ruby McCollum case for the *Pittsburgh Courier*, she moved to Fort Pierce, Florida, and continued working as a newspaper columnist and substitute teacher.

A stroke in 1959 landed her in the St. Lucie County Welfare Home where she died the following year. She was buried in an unmarked grave there until a resurgence of interest in her work brought her back into the classroom—not as a teacher but as the subject matter, taught alongside Toni Morrison and Maya Angelou.

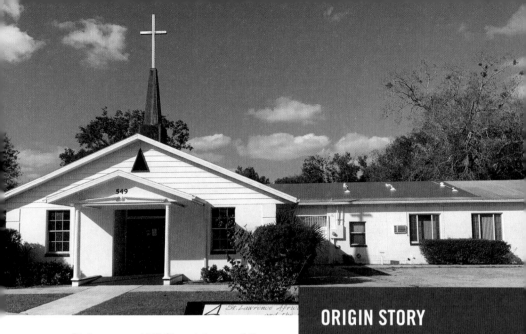

St. Lawrence AME Church is one of the stops along Eatonville's Zora Neale Hurston Trail. Photo by Joshua Ginsberg

Today, visitors follow Eatonville's Zora Neale Hurston Trail through historical markers and sites including the Zora Neale Hurston National Museum of Fine Arts. She is also celebrated in the town's annual Zora! Festival with events including public talks, conferences, movie screenings, and more.

ORIGIN STORY

WHAT: Eatonville's Zora Neale Hurston Trail

WHERE: A map and tour brochure is available from the museum at 344 E Kennedy Blvd., Eatonville.

COST: Walking or driving the trail is free.

PRO TIP: If you're feeling inspired and don't mind a bit of a road trip, you can continue along the Zora Neale Hurston Dust Tracks Heritage Trail in Fort Pierce.

Zora Neale Hurston lay in an unmarked grave in the Garden of Heavenly Rest Cemetery until Alice Walker (author of *The Color Purple*) located the site and ordered a headstone, identifying Hurston as a "Genius of the South."

PINEAPPLE EXPRESS

What happened to Orlando's prosperous pineapple industry?

If you are like most people, the answer to that question is typically, "Orlando had a pineapple industry?" The answer is yes, and you likely drive right through the former heart of the industry often on I-4. It all happened near the area of College Park and Ivanhoe Village just north of downtown where Orlando was once the largest pineapple producer in the entire country.

The history of Orlando's pineapples mainly dates back to 1885 when a man from Connecticut named George Russell moved to Florida. Once he settled in Orlando and had a thriving grain business, he bought a large plot of land near Lake Ivanhoe. That's where he began his pinery business and it boomed. His business survived occasional freezing temperatures and other environmental challenges, but he couldn't survive the growth of the

THE PINERY

WHAT: Restaurant at the site of former pineapple farm

WHERE: 295 NE Ivanhoe Blvd.

COST: The Michelin Guide gives it $$$.

PRO TIP: Get there early for an outside table for dinner or drinks. The sunset on Lake Ivanhoe is spectacular.

College Park isn't named after a university, but the streets are. Developer Walter Rose began naming streets after colleges and universities when he began building the Rosemere neighborhood in 1921. Yale, Princeton, Cornell, and Harvard are some of the originals.

The exterior of Russell's with the prominent pineapple on the sign. A sign inside the Pinery restaurant paying homage to Orlando's pineapple history. Photo by Sophia Brown

pineapple business from Cuba once trading was established. In the early 1900s he gave up on pineapples and switched his interest to a water amusement park named Joyland on Lake Ivanhoe. He later sold much of his property in 1919 for a subdivision named College Park to be developed.

If you drive the up-and-coming Ivanhoe Village area, you will still see memories of the pineapple industry. Restaurants like Russell's on Lake Ivanhoe have pineapples in their logo, while the Pinery has taken this history to the next level. Inside the Pinery you will find artifacts from this bygone era along with drinks and meals inspired by the local pineapple history.

ESCAPING THE DOLDRUMS

What's "Head Salesman" Trader Sam doing when he's not selling heads at Disney's Jungle Cruise?

Starting as early as 2 p.m. each day, a line of people in Hawaiian shirts begins forming outside a plain-looking door off the lobby of Disney's Polynesian Village Resort. If one didn't know any better, they might assume that after a full day at the theme parks, visitors have been conditioned to loiter in queues. Either that or the hotel has gone down to just one functioning restroom. Thankfully neither of those scenarios is the case, and for more than a few tikiphiles, the line is well worth the wait.

Opened in 2015, Trader Sam's Grog Grotto is the little-known Disney take on tiki. The Polynesian-themed decor is over the top in ways that would impress even Don Beach, from the tentacle wrapping itself around the bar shelf to the trinkets and treasures salvaged from the now-lost Adventurers Club. Look closely and you'll find enough Easter eggs to fill a dozen baskets, including a menu from the Rocketeer's South Seas Club, J. Thaddeus Toad's car keys hanging by the counter, a wooden sculpture of Lampie from *Pete's Dragon*, and plenty of references to *20,000 Leagues under the Sea*.

Then there are the drinks, many of which come in their own collectible mugs, such as the Nautilus, served in a submarine; the HippopotaMaiTai, which made a cameo appearance in an episode of *Loki*; and the Polynesian Pearl, which ever so rarely arrives in a black pearl. Ordering some of the different drinks will

---

For those seeking more of a true, vintage tiki experience, check out Aku Aku Tiki Bar along the southeastern corner of Lake Eola.

For attention to detail and decor, Trader Sam's Grog Grotto is hard to beat. Photo by Joshua Ginsberg

also unleash various animatronics and mini performances—just see what happens when you ask for a Zombie or an Uh-oa.

Not everything is on the menu either—just a few of these secret cocktails include Grunts Grog, the Heart of Polynesia (for all the *Moana* fans), and the Shipwreck on the Rocks.

FINDING CAPTAIN NEMO

WHAT: Trader Sam's Grog Grotto

WHERE: 1600 Seven Seas Dr., Lake Buena Vista

COST: Drinks with mugs can cost as much as $62. If that sounds crazy, you should see what some of those first-edition mugs fetch on eBay.

PRO TIP: If you'd rather skip the fanfare and the long wait, you can get the same drinks (and mugs) outside by the pool at Trader Sam's Tiki Terrace Restaurant.

AFRICAN SAFARI NEAR MAIN STREET USA

Where can you do an African safari in central Florida?

With a little Disney magic, you can do practically anything. So, if you want to see wild animals in their "natural" habitat, of course you can do that in Orlando.

Animal Kingdom at Walt Disney World Resort is all about the animals. But if you want an even closer view of the wildlife on the savanna, then you have to do the Wild Africa Trek. This is different from the Safari Tour that most people know about. The three-hour expedition starts off as a walking tour through the Kilimanjaro Forest with a personal guide. As the tour buses roll by beneath you, you get to walk across rope bridges to areas of the park that only the VIPs get to see. Once the walking tour is complete, you then get into a safari vehicle that takes a different path than the normal tour buses. This means you can stop and get close-up pictures of the antelopes, gazelles, and giraffes.

WILD AFRICA TREK AT ANIMAL KINGDOM

WHAT: An African safari in the middle of Walt Disney World

WHERE: 551 Rainforest Rd., Lake Buena Vista

COST: $199 on top of admission to the park

PRO TIP: You also get a photographer on your trip so you can relax while they snap all the pictures of your group.

Walt Disney picked central Florida over several locations to build his theme parks but he never saw them open. He chose the land and designed the parks but died four years before Magic Kingdom opened.

Disney's Animal Kingdom is a jungle paradise right in the middle of Florida with 2,000 animals from 300 different species. Photo by Mike Brown.

And just when you think the tour can't get any better, your tour bus driver takes you to a special dining area high on the savanna where you have a chef-prepared lunch overlooking the plains. It's doing Disney like very few people have ever done before. But be advised this tour does fill up early and it does cost extra.

MURALS WITH A MISSION

What's the significance of the monarch butterfly murals?

Both the quality and quantity of public artwork in Orlando is ever-increasing, especially when it comes to murals, which range from the eye-popping (like those in Lake Mary's mural alley), to the heart-stopping (as in the many Pulse-related murals, such as *Inspiration Orlando* by Michael Pilato and Yuriy Karabash). Within this continually evolving constellation, two murals produced by the Monarch Initiative deserve special recognition and a backstory.

Recognizing that the monarch butterfly has decreased from 4.5 million to fewer than 30,000 in a matter of decades, the Nature Conservancy set for itself the lofty ambition of raising awareness and trying to preserve the native milkweed that the butterflies use to lay their eggs. Florida is uniquely important for monarchs, as the only place on earth with both a year-round residential population as well as a migratory population that makes the multigenerational journey between Mexico and the United States.

To bring their vision to life, the Nature Conservancy partnered with Full Sail University and San Francisco–based Ink Dwell studio, which has been creating their own "migratory murals" throughout the country to highlight the plight of endangered and threatened wildlife. From the resulting creative chrysalis emerged two different murals. The first of these, titled *Milkweed*

If your taste in the arts is more theatrical, check out Orlando Shakes, which has been producing contemporary, classic, and children's plays in partnership with UCF (Orlando Shakespeare Theater, Inc.) since 1989.

Milkweed Galaxy *is one of two murals by the Monarch Initiative. Photo by Joshua Ginsberg*

Galaxy, was completed in February of 2018 at the Full Sail University campus in Winter Park. The second, *Midnight Dream*, came shortly after to occupy 3,500 square feet at the corner of Orange and Anderson, around the corner from the Dr. Phillips Center for the Performing Arts. Both murals depict monarchs on and around the milkweed upon which their existence depends.

While the murals make for stunning eye candy, the Monarch Initiative hopes that people will be inspired to do more than just take a selfie, and plant milkweed butterfly gardens in their own yards.

"TRAIN"ING THE GUESTS

Why did a train company build a hotel for workers in the middle of Winter Park?

Downtown Winter Park is one of the most exclusive areas in the entire metropolitan Orlando area. With its multimillion-dollar homes and upscale shops along Park Avenue, there is a historical gem hidden in plain sight. The Park Plaza Hotel at Park and New England Avenues is now a chic European-style hotel with distinctive greenery covering the balconies on the second floor. It has only 28 rooms and is luxury at its finest. But the origins of this building might surprise you.

The hotel was built back in 1922 as the city of Winter Park began growing as a popular winter getaway for northeasterners. The primary way to get to Florida around that time was by train, so work began in earnest to get the tracks to the Sunshine State, including downtown Winter Park. The Orlando & Winter Park Railway Company needed a place for their crews to stay, so they built the Hamilton Hotel to house them.

Once construction was completed, the workers moved out and the hotel opened to guests, many of whom were also coming to visit their children at Rollins College nearby. The luxurious lobby was flanked on both sides by glass rooms that were used for "sunning," so the people from up north could instantly feel the warmth of the Florida sun in the winter. Over

PARK PLAZA HOTEL

WHAT: Historic hotel right along Park Avenue

WHERE: 307 S Park Ave., Winter Park

COST: Rates vary, but websites list them around $200 a night.

PRO TIP: This is a great opportunity to feel "southern fancy." Book a hotel night and get there early. Spend the afternoon strolling along the shops on Park Avenue or take the boat tour nearby. Grab dinner at one of the amazing restaurants, then finish the evening with a bottle of wine on the balcony watching the people below.

Entrance to Park Plaza Hotel on luxurious Park Avenue in Winter Park. Photo by Sophia Brown

time, those rooms became small shops with iron doors inside that originated from a theater in New York City that was being torn down.

When the Spang family acquired the hotel in the 1970s, they upgraded the rooms to include their own original bathrooms, extended the balconies, and preserved much of the original timber in the lobby, but they kept the historic manually operated elevator from the Jacksonville Elevator Company. So, despite its humble beginnings, this now 100-year-old hotel stands as a testament to the resilience and affluence of the town in which it lies.

Winter Park was originally named Lakeview in 1858, then Osceola in 1870. In 1881, it was renamed Winter Park and the first college in Florida, Rollins College, was founded four years later in 1885.

MESSAGES HIDING IN PLAIN SIGHT

Ever feel like the city is trying to tell you something?

Lake Nona makes no secret of its love for innovative and local artwork—a quick drive around the lake will take you past both Tom Fruin's striking, prismatic *Glass House*, which looks a bit like a stained glass shed, and the pink tree, which was given new life by Cecilia Lueza. Maybe you'll stop to explore the 50,000-square-foot outdoor sculpture garden or notice the *Equinox* mural by Samantha's Walls gracing the Lake Nona Pixon apartment building.

When you're ready to stretch your legs or grab a bite to eat, head over to the large parking structure in Lake Nona Town Center. There you'll be treated to three more iconic artworks by local Filipino American artist Jefrë. The first and most visible of these is *The Beacon*, a six-story interactive landmark, which emits vibrant audio and visual effects. Its unusual, not-quite-cylindrical shape was inspired by René Laennec's original 1816 stethoscope—a heart attack requiring triple bypass surgery at age 35 gave the artist a new perspective on the fusion of medical technology and art.

A secret serenade: Back when Walt Disney World had its own airport facility, a set of grooves in the landing strip used to play "When You Wish upon a Star" when driven over at 45 miles per hour. Sadly, it sings no more—the grooves were removed in 2008.

Even if you don't cracking the code, The Beacon *and* Code Wall *are still dazzling interactive artworks. Photos by Joshua Ginsberg*

URBAN STEGANOGRAPHY

WHAT: *The Beacon* and *Code Wall*

WHERE: 6955 Lake Nona Blvd.

COST: Parking in the structure is subject to hourly rates.

PRO TIP: If you like unique, little-known artistic walls, check out *Mr. Imagination's Memory Wall* in Sanford, which could best be described as part outsider art-wall and part community time capsule.

The second artwork you'll find is *Disco*, gleaming in the sunlight. The angular, reflective surface of this 35-foot steel Labrador retriever was inspired by the rippling water of the area's namesake lake.

So where is the third piece? Look at the exterior of the parking structure itself and check out that unusual cut-out pattern of alternating circles and lines. Closer inspection will reveal that it's actually a nonrepeating pattern of ones and zeros—a code written in binary. You've found Jefrë's *Code Wall*, and the key to deciphering it is located outside the structure. Those willing to invest the time and brainpower in playing amateur cryptologist will be rewarded with inspirational messages from the artist.

AN ALL-INCLUSIVE STAY

How do you answer your kids' questions about racism while you're on vacation?

We all look forward to vacations as a time to disconnect from work laptops and phones and reconnect with family, but if you're traveling with children of a certain age, you know that you'll still have to respond to a whole lot of questions, not all of which are as easy to answer as, "Are we there yet?" If those questions happen to be on topics like racial inequality, you can find the answers you need at the Lake Nona Wave Hotel's one-of-a-kind social-justice-focused children's library.

Prior to the hotel's opening in December of 2021, management was looking for innovative programming when they came across edupreneur Pranoo Kumar Skomra's bookstore, Rohi's Readery, located in West Palm Beach, which is the first and only stand-alone children's bookstore dedicated to DEIA. They approached Pranoo about a collaboration, and she agreed to help curate what is now a collection of roughly 100 books from different marginalized communities, all of which are available to borrow or purchase. Some of the popular titles include *Papa, Daddy, and Riley* by Seamus Kirst, *Dear Black Boy* by Martellus Bennett, and *The Prince and the Frog* by Olly Pike. Guests can also listen to books and bedtime stories read aloud by Pranoo via the hotel's in-room iPads.

The hotel carries its commitment to diversity beyond the children's library, offering more than 200 different beverage brands supporting black-, female-, and LGBT-owned businesses.

A NEW WAVE

WHAT: The children's library inside the Lake Nona Wave Hotel

WHERE: 6100 Wave Hotel Dr.

COST: Member rates start around $316 per night.

PRO TIP: The library is inside the hotel's Living Room lobby game room, not in a separate, stand-alone room.

Lobby of the Lake Nona Wave Hotel. Photo by Joshua Ginsberg. Photo of Rohi's Readery owner Pranoo Kumar Skomra courtesy of the Lake Nona Wave Hotel.

Elsewhere in and around the hotel, guests will find other innovative features including some 500 original artworks, a sculpture garden featuring works from the Lewis Collection (one of the largest private art collections on earth), a Food Network—featured chef, and access to BEEP, which is one of the world's largest automated shuffle fleets.

Lake Nona is also home to the United States Tennis Association (USTA) National Campus and New Home of American Tennis. With 106 courts, it is currently ranked as the largest tennis complex in the country.

A BEAUTIFUL DAY IN THE NEIGHBORHOOD

Where and what did Fred Rogers study in college?

More than a decade before he achieved fame as the friendly and wise, cardigan-clad neighbor who imparted lessons in kindness, creativity, and community to millions of viewers, Fred McFeely Rogers was a student at Rollins College in Winter Park. He transferred there after one year at Dartmouth College and graduated magna cum laude with a bachelor of music and plans to attend seminary school. During his senior year in college though, he encountered something that altered his trajectory and brought him into ours. In 1951, he watched television at his parents' home and began to contemplate how this new medium could be used for the greater good. After graduating, he worked off-camera on multiple television shows until his big break came when the Canadian Broadcasting Corporation asked him to host a children's program called *Misterogers*.

In October of 2021, the college unveiled a tribute to its universally loved alumnus in the form of a bronze statue by British artist Paul Day titled *A Beautiful Day for a Neighbor*. It took the artist over 4,000 hours to complete the 3,000-pound statue, which stands over seven feet tall and shows a seated Mr. Rogers ringed by children, whom he amuses with his puppet Daniel Striped Tiger. Other puppets from the Neighborhood of

Other notable television and movie stars from Orlando include Wesley Snipes, Jonathan Jackson, Traylor Howard, and Bryana Salaz. Orlando's former city hall also deserves a mention for having been demolished (for real) in the opening scene of *Lethal Weapon 3*.

Make-Believe line the back of the statue, along with a line from the show's opening song.

Fred Rogers is a big name, but it's hardly the only one you will find on campus. Along the semicircular pathway surrounding the Mills Lawn is the Walk of Fame, which contains more than 500 stones, each inscribed with the name of a famous or historical figure. A short list of those represented includes Abraham Lincoln, Maya Angelou, Confucius, Thomas Edison, Martin Luther King Jr., Elizabeth Cady Stanton, Edmund Burke, and William Penn. At the western entrance to the walk is a millstone said to be roughly 300 years old, inscribed with the Shakespeare quote "Sermons in stone and good in everything."

ALL THE FEELS

WHAT: Mr. Rogers statue

WHERE: 1000 Holt Ave., Winter Park

COST: Free

PRO TIP: While you're looking at unusual statues and monuments in Winter Park, stop by Shady Park at Hannibal Square where the sculpture known as *Molecular Dog* sits and stays.

Fred Rogers immortalized in bronze, doing what he's best known for: entertaining and educating children. Photo by Joshua Ginsberg

VOYAGES TO SEE THE VIPS

Are the biggest houses in Orlando only visible by boat?

It is true that the city of Orlando has some magnificent mansions spread across the metro area. Some you may get a glimpse of through their massive entrances as you drive by, while others you will never see because they are hidden behind security guards in gated communities. But one way you can get to see them is on the water.

Take for example Shaquille O'Neal's former home on Lake Butler that was first listed for $28 million. Then you have perhaps the largest home in the area, a 50,000-square-foot megamansion visible primarily from Lake Dawn. And some of the most popular and historic are visible every day in Winter Park thanks to the Winter Park Boat Tour.

It is true that Winter Park was one of the first upper-crust residential areas in the city, so the magnificent homes often come with a story, which is where the boat captains come in. And since we live in Florida, the most exquisite parts of the homes are typically the entertaining areas in the back of the homes, near the water. As you cruise through the hidden canals connecting the lakes, you also get to see Florida wildlife that has lived here

WINTER PARK SCENIC BOAT TOUR

WHAT: An excursion around the Winter Park lakes

WHERE: 312 E Morse Blvd., Winter Park

COST: $16 for adults and $8 for children

PRO TIP: Do the tour during the holidays. The Winter Park Old Fashioned Christmas Cruise is a nighttime excursion where you get to see the magnificent homes on the lakes get decked out with the most amazing light displays you have ever seen.

The boarding docks for the Winter Park Scenic Boat Tours on Lake Osceola, not far from Park Avenue. Photo by Sophia Brown

for thousands of years, along with amazing views of Rollins College, and hear some name-droppings of those who live in the homes today.

Central Florida is home to more than 100 lakes, large and small. Three of the five biggest lakes in the state are here including Lake George (second), Lake Kissimmee (fourth), and Lake Apopka (fifth).

NO MAMA, NO PAPA, NO UNCLE SAM

What happened to the American and Filipino prisoners of war after the fall of the Bataan Peninsula in World War II?

For three months at the beginning of 1942, American and Filipino troops under General MacArthur had delayed the advance of the Japanese, but by March things looked increasing grim. From the Bataan Peninsula where his forces were consolidated, MacArthur vowed, "I shall return." He did make good on that promise two years later, but not before approximately one-quarter of the estimated 76,000 troops who were surrendered to Major General Nagano perished either at or en route to Camp O'Donnell. The 65-mile forced march they endured has achieved infamy as the Bataan Death March, along which troops were deprived of food and water and subjected to war-crime-qualifying treatment by their captors.

Fifty years later, Meandro de Mesa, a member of the Filipino-American community, became increasingly frustrated as Bataan and Corregidor slipped quietly from the collective memory. Memorials and monuments were erected to Vietnam, the Korean War, and other battles and conflicts, so de Mesa made it his personal mission to make sure that the Bataan Death March was among them.

There's another World War II–related monument in Lake Louisa State Park, which marks the spot where Lieutenant Dean R. Gilmore died after crashing his plane while leading a training flight. He was awarded the Distinguished Flying Cross for his 29 combat missions over Italy and Africa.

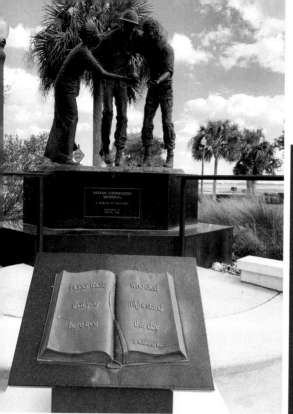

Sandra Mueller Storm's statue of a Filipino woman offering food to American and Filipino soldiers. Photo by Joshua Ginsberg

THE DEATH MARCH REMEMBERED

WHAT: The Bataan-Corregidor Memorial

WHERE: Lakefront Park, Kissimmee

COST: Free

PRO TIP: Those interested in Filipino history can find another monument at Lake Eola Park dedicated to Jose P. Rizal, whom it describes as the "architect of Filipino unity and the soul of the Philippine struggle for freedom and independence."

He partnered with Kissimmee City Commissioner Richard Herring and other residents, successfully raising enough money to commission sculptor Sandra Mueller Storm. Storm's haunting statue is of three figures: a Filipino soldier, supporting a limping American soldier, both of who are being offered a bowl of water by a Filipina woman (a kindness which cost some such women their lives).

The statue was unveiled on May 20, 1995, in a program that included a wreath laying and speeches from Philippine Brigadier General Tagumpay Nanadiego and retired US General Bruce Holloway. To some the memorial represents enduring friendship; to others it's a reminder of the horrors of war. For de Mesa, it is the crowning achievement of a lifetime.

MONUMENTALLY UNUSUAL

What is Kissimmee's most unique public monument (and tombstone)?

In the days following the bombing of Pearl Harbor, patriotism soared to new heights. Able-bodied Americans signed up in droves to serve the country abroad, while on the home front others found ways to support their communities. And in Kissimmee, one retired physician, Dr. Charles W. Bressler-Pettis, decided, for his part, to gather stones from each of the then 48 states and, with the help of his friend J. C. Fisher, transform them into a 50-foot-tall irregular step-pyramid. Of course, being the founder and president of Kissimmee's All-States Tourist Club might have given him a little additional incentive to build his monument to national unity.

Dr. Bressler-Pettis, impressed with his fellow club members' rock collections and possibly taking a page from the WPA's playbook in having constructed Minnesota's Fireplace of States, began reaching out for material, and the rocks came rolling in. Mayors, governors, even President Roosevelt sent a rock while cement was donated by local residents and businesses.

The resulting structure, weighing in at over 50 tons with steel reinforcement, is composed of roughly 1,500 rocks arranged into 21 tiers with colored panels, topped with an American flag. Along with the stones are some oddities such as buffalo horns from Montana, a petrified apple from Wisconsin, brain coral from

ROCKHOUNDING

WHAT: *The Monument of States*

WHERE: 300 E Monument Ave., Kissimmee

COST: Free

PRO TIP: If you look around you can find some mini monument street signs at various intersections. Most have been replaced, but a few are said to be the originals.

the Florida Keys, and two meteorites from Connecticut. Even after the monument was dedicated on March 28, 1943, rocks continued to arrive and found their way into the surrounding walkways.

The final contribution by Dr. Bressler-Pettis to the work was his own body. Following his death in 1954 as the result of injuries suffered from a fall "while working on a giant statue of a seeing-eye dog," Kissimmee made a one-time exception to its burial laws, allowing part of the doctor's remains to be entombed inside the monument.

In the 1950s, Dr. Bressler-Pettis and other merchants in downtown Kissimmee participated in annual beard contests to help promote the local rodeos. The Kissimmee Jaycees used the weeks leading up to the rodeos to raise money for charity by selling $1 shaving permits.

The oddly shaped Monument of States *in Kissimmee might be central Florida's most unique public rock collection. Photo by Joshua Ginsberg*

WHEN YOU WISH UPON A STAR

What uniquely whimsical and fantastic resort never charges its visitors a single dollar for their stay?

Henri Landwirth understood what it was like to lose one's childhood. Born in Belgium in 1927, he spent most of his teenage years surviving the Nazi death camps Auschwitz and Mauthausen. He arrived in the United States with just 20 dollars to his name, was drafted into the army during the Korean War, and then used the GI Bill to take a course in hotel management. By 1954 he was managing the Starlite Motel in Cocoa Beach, Florida, where he befriended the Mercury Seven astronauts staying at the property. In the 1980s he began offering free hotel rooms to critically ill children through the Make-A-Wish Foundation. When Amy, a young girl with leukemia, passed away before travel arrangements could be completed, Landwirth vowed that never again would a child be failed in this way on his watch, and when a Holocaust survivor uses that phrase, you know they mean it.

He set about building a unique vacation village, which has grown to 89 acres and 166 villas, where children and their families can be transported within 24 hours. Today it serves as a wish-fulfillment center for some 250 different wish-granting organizations, where more than 177,000 families from around the world have had a once-in-a-lifetime experience.

Beyond its dedicated staff, replete with character actors, it features a Castle of Miracles with a magic

Elmer the Tree, Henri's Starlite Scoops and the Castle of Miracles are just a few of the spots that bring magic to children and their families. Photos by Joshua Ginsberg

forest; a gurgling, burping wishing well; an enchanted carousel; and a fairy who affixes children's personalized stars to the ceiling each night. There's a dinosaur-themed miniature golf course with a glowing cave, a massive Candyland-inspired playground, a movie theater, pony rides, Elmer the anthropomorphic slumbering tree, fishing ponds, and anything else a kid could dream of. And there is ice cream. Henri's Starlite Scoops serves ice cream all day every day.

Give Kids the World Village has a deep relationship with Hasbro. While you won't see the company advertised directly on the property, you will see a life-size Candyland board running through the playground there and a specially created My Little Pony named Twinkle Hope.

A SWEET DEAL ON SWAMPLAND

What became of Hamilton Disston's ventures and investments in central Florida?

The year was 1881 and Florida had a problem: it was short the million dollars it owed its bondholders. Enter wealthy Philadelphian Hamilton Disston, heir to his family's saw manufacturing business. Four years earlier, on a fishing trip with Henry Shelton Sanford, Disston realized the fortune that could be made by draining and developing central Florida's mosquito-infested swampland. So he bought it. All of it. Four million acres, to be exact (about a third of the available land in the state at the time).

From Disston's land rose the cities of St. Cloud, Kissimmee, Tarpon Springs, and Gulfport (once called Disston City). It also allowed both Henry Plant and Henry Flagler to lay train tracks deeper into the state. While Disston's dredging efforts met with mixed results, his small sugar plantation got off to a promising start. He expanded from 20 acres of sugar fields in 1886 to 1,800 acres within just two years. Disston constructed a full-scale sugar factory, yielding 5,000 pounds of granulated sugar per acre. Furthermore, in 1890, congress enacted a bounty for sugar producers to boost domestic production. The company grew, despite management problems, floods, and other challenges. It looked like Disston

A ruined brick structure is all that remains today of Hamilton Disston's sugar mill. Photo by Joshua Ginsberg

might achieve a level of commercial success that earlier sugar mill owners had only dreamed of.

So what happened? The Panic of 1893, which closed thousands of businesses and banks. Congress ended the sugar bounty it had been paying out, and Disston watched his nascent empire dissolve. Ultimately he mortgaged his Florida holdings and returned to Philadelphia where he spent the last two years of his short life.

Today the crumbling brick ruins of Disston's sugar mill sit mostly forgotten and overgrown in St. Cloud—a cautionary reminder of how quickly the taste of sweet success can come to a bitter end.

If you're craving more sweet history nearby, you can also check out the Dummett Sugar Mill Ruins, the Cruger-dePeyster Plantation Sugar Mill Ruins, and the Dunlawton Sugar Mill Gardens (which is now a botanical garden populated by the leftover dinosaur statues from Bongoland).

OIA VERSUS MCO

Why does Orlando's primary airport have the call letters MCO but is called OIA?

Orlando International Airport has grown into one of the busiest airports in the world thanks in large part to our booming tourist industry, a growing metropolis, and a robust business sector. When most people say they are going to the airport, they use the abbreviation O-I-A, which makes sense since it's Orlando International Airport. But when you check on a flight or get your bag tag, there it is, the three letters that seem to make no sense: MCO. Those three letters are actually a big part of our area's history and symbolize one of our most famous aviators.

MCO is the airport designator code for the former McCoy Air Force Base, named after Colonel Michael McCoy. McCoy was a veteran pilot in a town that was a center for aviation at the time. The colonel was based at the then Pinecastle Air Force Base on the day he was piloting a B-47 Stratojet when something went wrong. As he was zipping above College Park, flames could be seen from the jet's engine as he was able to steer the jet away from a neighborhood and crashed into a field near Lee Road and Orange Blossom Trail, killing him and three others onboard on McCoy's 52nd birthday.

HEMISPHERE RESTAURANT AT THE HYATT

WHAT: Ninth-floor restaurant with dramatic views of the entire airfield

WHERE: Hyatt Regency Orlando International Airport, 9th Floor, 9300 Jeff Fuqua Blvd.

COST: Open Table lists prices from $31 to $50.

PRO TIP: There is also a restaurant at the Hyatt called McCoy's, named after the colonel. This one is great for a quick meal before a flight.

The air force first blamed McCoy for the crash, while others thought it might have been sabotage. Others said the plane malfunctioned. Colonel McCoy, after all, was a superstar pilot and the United States was in the midst of the Cold War. Once the report was released about 50 years later, the cause was listed as "operator error." Regardless, aviation was center stage in central Florida and the military wanted to honor his memory, so Pinecastle was renamed McCoy Air Force Base. It was later changed to Orlando International Airport, but it's still symbolized with MCO.

Art in odd places: If you're passing through the airport and see a guy sleeping in a glass enclosure, don't worry about waking him up. That's one of artist Duane Hanson's hyperrealistic sculptures known as *The Traveler* (see next page), and he's been napping through flights there since 1986.

Photo by John Brown

TERMINALLY CREATIVE

Shouldn't somebody wake that guy up before he misses his flight?

Sayings like "The journey is the destination" might have sounded pretty wise when you first heard them, but they're probably about the last thing on your mind while wheeling your baggage through Orlando International Airport. If you can resist the urge to just dash through it as quickly as possible on your way to your hotel or your gate, you might be rewarded with something fascinating that millions pass by without ever noticing.

Sometimes, of course, we have no choice but to slow down—delays and cancellations have become an all-too-common feature of air travel. Such would seem to be the plight of the mustached, middle-aged man in the orange shirt taking a little nap surrounded by his luggage in the Terminal A concourse between the east and west security gates. But how did he manage to end up behind a glass enclosure?

Whatever flight he was waiting for departed long ago—he's been camped out there since 1986. Don't worry though, he's got nowhere else to be—he's actually a polyester resin and fiberglass statue titled *The Traveler*, created by artist Duane Hanson, who made a name for himself with his hyperrealistic, life-size sculptures of ordinary people doing mundane things.

The Traveler may be on an eternal layover, but at least he's in good company. There's *Leoguana Da Vinci* in Terminal B with shimmering mosaic tiles for scales, and Terminal C has its new *Windows on Orlando*, an immersive digital storytelling wall.

Another unique public artwork that visitors often miss while traveling is the one-of-a-kind, Mickey Mouse electrical pylon along I-4 in Celebration.

The Traveler *has been sleeping through flights for more than 35 years. Photo by Joshua Ginsberg*

Recently it featured works by the Highwaymen—a group of self-taught Black landscape artists who decided to show their works along US Highway 1 after being excluded from the museums and galleries. There are plenty of other artworks as well alongside cultural and historical displays, certainly enough to make curious travelers pause while passing through.

ART IN ODD PLACES

WHAT: Art and culture on display at the Orlando International Airport (MCO)

WHERE: 1 Jeff Fuqua Blvd.

COST: Free

PRO TIP: While you're at the MCO, Hemisphere restaurant inside the Hyatt connected to the airport is a frequently overlooked and reasonably priced spot for a date night.

CARVING OUT A PLACE FOR ONESELF

Who was the most famous sculptor to live in Sanford?

Those driving or walking down Osceola Avenue in Sanford may catch sight of an unusual artwork—what appears to be a figure chiseling itself from a block of stone. That piece, titled *Man Carving His Own Destiny*, is likely Albin Polasek's most famous and his most directly self-referential work of art. This version stands in the front yard of the artist's studio-cum-museum, a true hidden gem that reflects Polasek's unique story and vision.

That story begins in Frenstat, Moravia (now the Czech Republic), where the artist was born in 1879. Despite showing tremendous artistic talent, it took a few different apprenticeships for him to find the right fit as a wood-carver. In 1901 he followed his brothers to the United States and continued his training at the Pennsylvania Academy of Fine Arts, where he learned classical sculpting techniques from Charles Grafly. Winning the Prix de Rome sent him abroad for a three-year fellowship, after which he set up shop in New York and produced hundreds of extraordinary works including the *Masaryk Monument* in Chicago, the *Woodrow Wilson Monument* in Prague, *Radegast* in the Frenstat Town Hall, and many others.

In 2022, the Polk Museum of Art hosted an exhibition of work by another world-famous sculptor: Auguste Rodin. Featuring more than 40 works by the French artist, it was the largest installation of sculpture in the museum's history.

Visitors can tour Polasek's home and studio. Photo by Joshua Ginsberg

WHAT: The Albin Polasek Museum & Sculpture Gardens

WHERE: 633 Osceola Ave., Winter Park

COST: $12 for adults, $10 for seniors and college students, $7 for K-12 students; members get in free.

PRO TIP: Can you find the artist's own likeness in one of the 14 panels of his *Stations of the Cross*? Look for the man sporting a decidedly nonbiblical-style mustache.

In 1950 Polasek became a septuagenarian, moved to Winter Park, and married his friend and former student Ruth Sherwood. What should have been a blissful period became a difficult and tragic one. First, Polasek suffered a stroke that paralyzed the left side of his body, and then, 22 months after the wedding, Sherwood died. Polasek continued to work, completing another 18 major works with his right hand and assistance. He also remarried in 1961 to Emily Muska Kubat, who was instrumental in preserving Polasek's studio and legacy. Be sure to wander through the gardens as well, where mythical figures, flora, and fauna all share the 3.5-acre property around Lake Osceola.

GEMÜTLICHKEIT IN SANFORD

What is *gemütlichkeit* and where can you find it in the Orlando area?

Florida is about 4,700 miles from Germany, and it takes about 10 hours to fly from OIA to the airport in Dusseldorf. But if you would rather make a short drive to Sanford, you will see German culture and food at its finest right here in central Florida. For years, people have wondered why an authentic German restaurant has such a massive following in a suburban town.

Hollerbach's German Restaurant is legendary, and the legend has continued to grow since Theo and Linda Hollerbach opened the establishment in 2001, based on the phrase "The place where gemütlichkeit happens." That basically means a place of coziness and belonging. And they have created gemütlichkeit in Sanford, as the restaurant is often named one of the top German beer halls in America by national travel magazines. As the years went by, Hollerbach's went from a quaint little restaurant to a quaint BIG destination. It's so popular that you often meet people from Germany at the restaurant who stop by to check it out while in Florida on vacation.

In addition to the authentic German food, you can also dance along with the oompah-pah band most nights of the week. The restaurant has grown from the original restaurant into an

Sanford was once the "big town" in central Florida thanks to the St. Johns River and Lake Monroe. You can still experience Florida as it used to be aboard the nearby rivership *Barbara-Lee*, which is an authentic paddleboat that does daily cruises on the St. Johns River.

Hollerbach's Willow Tree Cafe in downtown Sanford is known around the world for amazing German food and entertainment. Photo by Sophia Brown

expansive beer hall, a rooftop party deck, and now even an art gallery. However, if you plan on going on a weekend, you need to make a reservation about two weeks in advance, depending on the size of your entourage. Otherwise, you might be standing for an hour watching everyone else doing the polka.

HOLLERBACH'S WILLOW TREE RESTAURANT

WHAT: Authentic German restaurant and entertainment

WHERE: 205 E 1st St., Sanford

COST: Yelp rates it at $$

PRO TIP: October is the perfect time to check out downtown Sanford. Along with the slightly cooler temps in the evenings, the Oktoberfest celebration is legendary.

HAUL OF FAME

What did garbage trucks look like 20, 50, and 100 years ago?

While most folks try to refrain from "talking trash," for Scott Collier, curator of the Waste Pro Garbage Truck Museum, that's actually a big part of his job these days—talking to visitors and children about the more than 30 fully restored garbage trucks housed next to the company's main building. It's a labor-intensive endeavor to bring these vehicles up to museum quality, costing as much as $60,000 each. To some, that might seem like a waste of a good investment, but for Waste Pro, investing in waste—or more specifically, its safe and efficient removal—is an essential feature of the company's culture.

The museum evolved from the private collection of Waste Pro founder and chairman John Jennings, who wanted to preserve and pass on the history of waste removal for future generations. That industry goes back over a century to the coal trucks that were asked by their clients to return and remove the ash and

RECYCLED AND RESTORED

WHAT: The Waste Pro Garbage Truck Museum

WHERE: 3705 St. Johns Pkwy., Sanford

COST: Free

PRO TIP: Call ahead to schedule a visit and go earlier in the day if you can—the garage is not air-conditioned and it can get a bit steamy.

The Orlando Auto Museum at Dezerland Park is another place to find rare and one-of-a-kind vehicles. Its collection includes a Ghostbusters Ecto 1, James Bond screen-used vehicles, Batmobiles, and the world's longest super limo, which measures over 100 feet long.

One truck you won't see in the museum is an exceedingly rare 1950s Roto-Pac Escalator/Compactor. Jennings dreams of acquiring one, but until he does so, you can find it in one of the museum-produced coloring books.

rubbish. Visitors can find one of these earliest forms of garbage trucks, a 1925 Mack AC Dunn coal truck restored alongside a 1922 Mack AB Leach Ford Refuse Getter, a 1930s DeMartini, a 1975 White Dempster Front Loader, and many others grouped into three rooms according to decade.

Other unique points of interest in the museum include two trucks from the Denzel Washington film *Fences*. Unlike the restored trucks, these ones started off brand new and the Waste Pro team was tasked with making them look realistically aged and worn. There's also a one-of-a-kind prototype Murphy Refuse-Packer and a miniature version, with the patent, in the museum's library.

With scavenger hunts set up for kids and plenty of displays and documents to explore, you might find yourself agreeing that one man's trash trucks are another's treasure.

TRANSCENDENCE IN OPALESCENCE

Where can you find the most comprehensive collection of work by Louis Comfort Tiffany?

Whether you're fascinated by the beauty and craftsmanship of Louis Comfort Tiffany glasswork or you're looking for the most appropriate place to seek divine inspiration, the Charles Hosmer Morse Museum of American Art has something you won't want to miss. Within its spectacular collection of Tiffany glasswork is one very special piece—the chapel interior Tiffany designed for the 1893 World's Columbian Exposition in Chicago.

For the chapel, Tiffany drew on medieval and Byzantine styles but did not have a specific church as his model in creating what is essentially one massive sculptural glass mosaic. Though the arches and columns are relatively simple, the intricacy and patterns within patterns on every reflective surface are dazzling. The gaze of viewers flows from the altar up the steps and onward, up to the 1,000-pound, eight-by-ten-foot cruciform "electrolier" and stained glass pieces overhead. The overall effect is akin to being transported to the inner sanctum of some mystical, celestial city—which is more or less precisely what it was designed for.

After awing millions in "the White City," the chapel was reassembled in the basement crypt of the Cathedral of St. John the Divine in New York. There it gradually fell into disuse and disrepair, until Tiffany arranged to reclaim his masterpiece and install it at

If you love Tiffany glass artwork enough to drive 100 miles for it, take a trip to St. Augustine and feast your eyes on the 79 original stained glass windows in the dining hall at Flagler College.

The Tiffany Chapel, restored and resplendent. Photo by Joshua Ginsberg

Laurelton Hall (his estate in Long Island). After Tiffany's death in 1933, for a time Laurelton Hall was preserved by Tiffany's own foundation, but by 1946 financial difficulties made the upkeep untenable. Much of the contents of the mansion was sold or destroyed in a fire in 1957.

Enter Jeannette and Hugh McKean, who committed themselves in 1959 to salvaging all they could from the old estate, including the leaded-glass windows, some of the doors, and the chapel, all of which they brought back to their museum in Winter Park.

A TIFFANY EPIPHANY

WHAT: The Tiffany Chapel inside the Charles Hosmer Morse Museum of American Art

WHERE: 445 N Park Ave., Winter Park

COST: $6 for adults, $5 for seniors, $1 for students, and free for children under 12. November through April, Fridays from 4 to 8 p.m. are also free to the public.

PRO TIP: One evening each year at the start of the holiday season, the museum presents the Bach Festival Choir and Brass Ensemble for a concert in Winter Park's Central Park, featuring illuminated Tiffany glass windows.

A HORSE IS A HORSE, OF COURSE, OF COURSE

Who has the honor of being the only nonhuman buried in Sanford's Lakeview Cemetery?

In 1877, the city of Sanford was incorporated as part of Henry Shelton Sanford's grand plan to build a transportation hub and gateway between South Florida and the rest of the county. A short seven years later, Sanford's eponymous community had grown enough to necessitate adding a cemetery and funeral home. Just as Sanford saw potential in situating his city to meet the needs of travelers, in 1884, T. J. Miller found opportunity in helping residents reach their final destinations as the city's first undertaker. He didn't do so alone though—he had his gray workhorse, Bob, to rely on.

Born in 1877, Bob became the Miller family horse and for 28 years took local residents on their final ride to Miller's Lakeview Cemetery. Regardless of color or creed, at a time when segregation was still the law of the land, Bob went about his work admirably. So much so that when Bob expired, Miller ran an obituary in the local paper and had his faithful companion buried in his own plot, making Bob the only nonhuman resting in the cemetery. The tombstone was replaced in 1980 after it was damaged, but it still stands alone, apart from the other graves, and is the only tombstone facing the road where Bob worked in life.

If you'd rather visit living animals, the Central Florida Zoo (formerly the Sanford Municipal Zoo) is nearby. The zoo has been there for over a century now, which makes it something of an endangered species itself as one of the oldest running attractions in central Florida.

Bob is the subject of a small display inside the Sanford Museum. Photo by Joshua Ginsberg

original tombstone, purchased by his owner ...er, was found during the renovation of the ...er's lodge at Evergreen Cemetery. ... stone had been struck by a car and damaged ...unt Monument Co. donated the new stone.

ON TO GREENER PASTURES

WHAT: The grave of Bob the horse

WHERE: 1900 State Hwy. 46 A, Sanford

COST: Both the cemetery and the Sanford Museum are free to visit.

PRO TIP: Be prepared to share the road, there are occasional reports of drivers unexpectedly encountering with Bob's ghost near the cemetery.

That the horse has been referred to alternatively as Bob, Big Bob, and Old Bob can create some confusion, especially since Old Bob was also the name of the horse who drew President Lincoln's hearse. While the final whereabouts of that particular Old Bob are unknown, there's probably no connection between the two horses, as Miller's horse wasn't born until 12 years after Lincoln's assassination. Regardless of presidential pedigree, you can leave flowers, oats, apples, or horseshoes at Bob's grave in Sanford.

THE FORGOTTEN FLORIDA CANAL

Why was the canal across Florida abruptly shut down?

Most people are well aware of the 50-mile-long Panama Canal in Central America. But a project twice that length was started in Florida yet abandoned after a fraction of the project was completed. It's called the Cross Florida Barge Canal, and parts of the project are still very visible today.

The idea of a canal across northern Florida dates back centuries as shippers looked for a quicker way to get from the Gulf of Mexico to the Atlantic Ocean. The New Deal program in the 1930s gave life to the proposal as millions of dollars were allocated for projects to put Americans back to work during the Great Depression. Money for the projects ran out three years later, and it sat dormant until 1964 when President Lyndon B. Johnson arrived in Palatka to officially break ground for the project.

Dredging began, dams were built, and hills were moved as the canal finally started coming to life. But the 1960s were also a time of enlightenment for environmental affairs, so President Richard Nixon put the project on hold in 1971 even though more than $70 million had already been spent on the canal. It was ultimately killed in 1990 as congress deauthorized the project, which eventually became part of the

MARJORIE HARRIS CARR CROSS FLORIDA GREENWAY

WHAT: Hiking trail along proposed route of canal

WHERE: 8282 SE Hwy. 314, Ocala

COST: The trail and park are free.

PRO TIP: This historic part of the trail can be a bit uneven. If you are looking for smoother sections to walk or ride your bike, those can be accessed across central Florida.

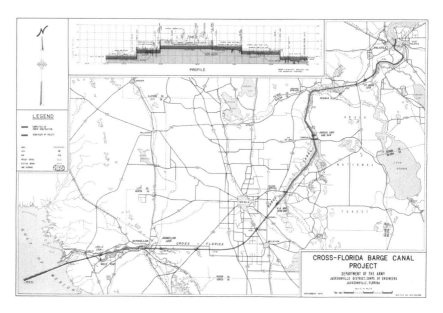

Map of the original plan for the Cross-Florida Barge Canal. Portions of the project were completed, but the project was eventually killed.

Cross Florida Greenway. It became the most expensive public works project in US history that was never completed.

There are two completed sections, including the initial section in central Florida, which includes the waterway formed by the Rodman Dam. Much of the original path has now been converted into Marjorie Harris Carr Cross Florida Greenway, which meanders along the route that the canal would have taken if finished.

If you really want to go looking for secret history, there are still eerie-looking bridge supports that were erected in the woods near Ocala along the trail for a bridge designed to go across the massive waterway. There is another bridge support in the median of US 441 in Santos.

FOREVER UNDER THE HAPPY LITTLE CLOUDS

Where was America's favorite television artist laid to rest?

Few who have chosen to make central Florida their final resting place receive as much posthumous love as Robert Norman Ross. Immediately recognizable for his bushy Afro haircut and tranquil voice, he brought landscape speed-painting into the lives of millions via his show, *The Joy of Painting*, which aired from 1983 until 1994 on PBS.

How he came to spend eternity at Woodlawn Cemetery in Gotha is not the result of some "happy accident." The painter was born in Daytona Beach and returned to Florida upon retiring from the United States Air Force. While serving at Eielson Air Force Base in Alaska, he came across Bill Alexander's show, *The Magic of Oil Painting*, and adopted the alla prima (or "wet-on-wet") style. Eventually the supplemental income he made from these paintings eclipsed his military paycheck. Once he retired at the rank of master sergeant, which entailed a lot of barking orders at subordinates, he decided he never wanted to raise his voice again.

He went on to study and partner with Alexander before striking off on his own. Over the course of his life, he produced an estimated 30,000 paintings. That number could have been vastly higher if he hadn't died of complications of lymphoma on July 4, 1995, at the age of only 52.

Another way to appreciate the artwork of Bob Ross is to visit the Bob Ross Gallery and Workshop in a strip mall in New Smyrna Beach. There you can take a class and find inspiration in their 59 original Bob Ross paintings.

Visitors often leave personal and creative tributes at the grave of Bob Ross. Photo by Joshua Ginsberg

NO PRESSURE

WHAT: The grave of Bob Ross

WHERE: 400 Woodlawn Cemetery Rd., Gotha

COST: Free

PRO TIP: When visiting this or any burial place, heed the artist's words and "be a gentle whisper."

Now 26 years after his death, Ross is experiencing a surge in popularity. Perhaps it's a result of so many people seeking new hobbies during the recent COVID-19 pandemic. Or maybe it's his calm, reassuring words that people crave. Whatever the reasons, if you wish to pay a visit to his grave, you'll usually find his headstone under a heap of offerings ranging from brushes and palette knives to flowers, personal messages, cigarettes, soda bottles, beer cans, and plenty of paintings.

PRESIDENTS HALL OF FAME

How can I experience Washington, DC, without leaving central Florida?

If you have always wanted to see what the Oval Office looks like but didn't want to run for president or make the trip to Washington, DC, then head to Clermont. The Presidents Hall of Fame is a fascinating tribute to all the things that make our government one of a kind. This is not just a roadside attraction where you take a few pictures and then drive down the road. This is a history lesson like you have never experienced before. There are plenty of exhibits to keep the kids entertained, along with tons of historical information so adults can learn as well. There is even a 1,200-square-foot replica of the White House so you can get a closer look at all the rooms of the executive mansion.

But that is just the beginning. This attraction actually evolved from a wax museum called the House of Presidents and kept on growing thanks to its owner, John Zweifel, who died in 2020. So you can see up close and personal how our presidents and first ladies actually looked in person.

And some of the displays give you a look at history that you wouldn't think would be as impactful as they are. You can see a seat from the Ford Theater where President Lincoln was shot by an assassin. It's odd how artifacts from our national history

PRESIDENTS HALL OF FAME

WHAT: Museum dedicated to US presidents

WHERE: 123 Hwy. 27, Clermont

COST: $15 for adults, $8 for students

PRO TIP: There is also plenty of Disney and Florida history on-site as well, so there is a little something for everyone.

The Presidents Hall of Fame is a wealth of knowledge about our leaders. Even President Ronald Reagan stopped by for a visit. Top photo by John Brown. Inset photo courtesy of the Presidents Hall of Fame

can impact you, but seeing them in person truly gives you a new perspective on what makes our country so unique.

President Ronald Reagan once called this place a "national treasure," so you can see the bar is set pretty high. There is even a replica of Mount Rushmore outside! The Discovery Channel also thought this attraction was worth an entire show, so it's obviously worth a trip to Lake County to explore.

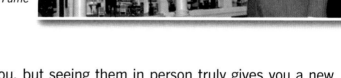

Even President Ronald Reagan was impressed by this museum. According to the museum, Reagan called it a "true national treasure."

OFF-ROADING IN THE FLORIDA OUTBACK

Why is a 16-foot-tall school bus the best way to explore Florida?

If ever there was a quintessential Florida attraction, it would have to have orange groves, alligators, exotic animals, and a monster truck. And that is exactly what you get at Showcase of Citrus when you take the monster truck tour. This is truly one of those "Only in Florida" roadside attractions that you have to check out.

The monster trucks are actually modified school buses that are 16 feet tall, 40 feet long, and 14 feet wide, which give you a view of Florida nature and citrus like none other. Think of the trip as part nature, part thrill ride, and part history lesson, all rolled into one.

These massive vehicles take you off road for an excursion over the 2,500-acre working ranch and farm that you won't forget. Sure, you'll get to explore native woodlands and citrus groves all while keeping a sharp eye out for giant Bigfoot, wood fairies, and friendly gnomes! And if you want a bit more backwoods Florida, that's where these monster trucks are at their finest. Their massive tires glide effortlessly through exotic animal enclosures where you can see the gators . . . from a safe distance above

---

About 15 miles north of this farm is an unexpected find in Florida. Lakeridge Winery has won numerous awards and bills itself as the "center of the state's grape industry." The wines are made from muscadine grapes, which are known as the "super fruit of the South" because of their high antioxidant levels and anti-inflammatory properties.

WARNING!
Now Entering
BIG-FOOT
TERRITORY

Giant school buses take you through the property so you can see the Florida environment like never before. Photo courtesy of Showcase of Citrus.

them! And just for added fun, you'll also get to see some zebras, water buffalo, watusi, American bison, longhorn cattle, and exotic birds throughout the ranch. And when you are done with the nature tour, you can do some shopping at the Old Time Country Store.

SHOWCASE OF CITRUS

WHAT: 2,500-acre estate with outdoor activities

WHERE: 15051 Frank Jarrell Rd., Clermont

COST: Picking costs vary. Monster truck tours are $25 for adults and $15 for kids. Petting zoo and mining activity also cost additional.

PRO TIP: This is one of those attractions that must be on your list for when family visits from up north. There is so much "old Florida" all rolled into one that they will never forget the trip.

THE I-4 EYESORE

Will it ever be finished?

Things that make a building noteworthy might include its historical significance, architecture, innovative design, unconventional building materials, famous residents, and so forth. None of these, however, are what the 18-story, 300,000-square-foot Majesty Building is known for. Its unusual claim to fame? That it has been under construction for over two decades with still no end in sight.

When Claud Bowers, CEO of the religious television station WACX Super Channel 55, first revealed his plan to construct the retail and broadcast facility (which, with its steel-gray curvature, looks a bit like an homage to HVAC ductwork), it seemed ambitious but feasible. Certainly his goal of erecting the building without incurring any debt sounded pretty good. As it heads into its 22nd year of casting a partially completed shadow over the interstate highway, the cost has surpassed $40 million, leading more than a few to suggest that the building would have already been completed (and for less than the cost of the taxes) had the owner just taken out a loan.

UNDER CONSTRUCTION

WHAT: The Majesty Building

WHERE: 123 E Central Pkwy., Altamonte Springs

COST: Far more than expected (but free to gawk at)

PRO TIP: Man plans, God laughs.

Central Florida does actually have plenty of fully completed architectural marvels. The Innovation, Science, and Technology Building at Florida Polytechnic University by architect Santiago Calatrava is one of them, and the FSU "Child of the Sun" campus designed by Frank Lloyd Wright is another.

The Majesty Building in its current, incomplete state along I-4.
Photo by Joshua Ginsberg

Construction began in early 2001 but stalled out, leaving the exposed interior for those driving past to view and poke fun at. During this 10-year stretch, it was given the nickname by which most know it today, "the I-4 eyesore." Construction resumed in 2018 and glass windows have since enclosed the structure, which Bowers claimed would be finished in 12 months, then 18 months, then at some indeterminate point in the future. The I-4 Ultimate lane expansion project has been cited as the latest cause of delays.

Perhaps one day Bowers's building will broadcast the word of God, but until such time, it can instead serve as proof positive that "God's work on earth is never done." At least not along I-4.

OF PACHYDERMS AND PARKS

How did a waterskiing elephant pave the way for a beloved park?

One of the most popular state parks in the area is best known for a restaurant where you get to cook your own pancakes. But the history behind the quiet De Leon Springs State Park is anything but quiet. It first became a tourist attraction in the late 1800s but really gained in popularity in the 1920s when the Ponce de Leon Springs Hotel and Casino opened near the spring that some though might be the "fountain of youth." As cars became more common, it transitioned into a roadside park in 1953. That was when a waterskiing elephant was the star of the park, long before the pancakes stole the show.

The elephant was named Queenie and rode through the water with Liz Dane on a giant platform, allowing them to ski together. Liz's father had bought the elephant as a baby to be a part of this uniquely Florida attraction. The elephant was only a part of the show for about three years, but the park itself remained popular with a jungle cruise, tropical gardens, and other attractions for the next 16 years.

The park was purchased by government agencies in 1982 and became De Leon Springs State Park. That is when the old sugar mill was put back into service as the Old Sugar Mill Pancake House, where guests were able to cook the flapjacks

COOKING UP SOME HISTORY

WHAT: De Leon Springs State Park

WHERE: 601 Ponce Deleon Blvd., De Leon Springs

COST: $6 per vehicle to enter the park. Yelp gives the restaurant a $ rating.

PRO TIP: Don't wait to get reservations. It fills up fast, so stop by the restaurant before you explore De Leon Springs.

Liz Dane waterskiing with Queenie the Elephant in 1958 at what is now De Leon Springs State Park. Courtesy of Liz Dane

right at their own table. It's come a long way since Queenie ruled the park, but you can still see old Florida at its finest with a hike in the "jungle" or a dip in the 72-degree springs that will keep you forever young.

MOUNT DORA CATACOMBS

Why did wealthy residents of Mount Dora build an underground bunker?

In the buildup to the Cold War, Americans were worried about a nuclear war between the United States and Russia. Due to those concerns, families across the country built "atomic bomb shelters" in their backyards as a place to move underground and escape the toxic fallout. Some of the wealthier residents of Mount Dora took that to a different level and constructed an underground shelter that was big enough to house 25 families for six months.

The massive group survival shelter was the idea of the Lake County Health Director, Dr. James Hall. The 5,000-square-foot shelter was constructed in 1961 for about $60,000. Building the structure underground in Florida was a massive undertaking, but so was keeping it a secret. The family that owned the land told neighbors that they were simply building a croquet court so as to not arouse suspicions. It took only six months to construct despite needing a 6,000-gallon fuel tank, a 4,000-gallon water tank, a backup power grid, and massive dehumidifiers that were needed to keep mold from growing. The entrance to the compound was disguised inside a shed.

Even though you won't be able to access the catacombs, you should still make the trip to Mount Dora. This is one of the best small towns in America with a street festival seemingly every weekend and has been called "The Festival City." Its quaint downtown and cute lakeside houses have also earned the town the nickname "The New England of the South."

Mt. Dora Yacht Club House,   Mt. Dora, Fla.

Historical images of downtown Mount Dora. Wealthy members of the small town built a hidden bunker during the Cold War.

MOUNT DORA CATACOMBS

WHAT: Hidden underground bunker

WHERE: Only a few people still know.

COST: Not an option!

PRO TIP: Don't bother asking where it is. The people who know won't tell.

Each family had a room they stocked with everything they might need for six months. That included toys, clothing, books, and anything else deemed necessary to pass the time underground. There were communal spaces where families could mingle and eat. There was even a medical clinic. Interestingly, the bunker was only used once! The families did a "dress rehearsal" to make sure everything worked correctly. But as relations between the two countries thawed, the structure began to deteriorate with many of the items still in the rooms. The catacombs are regarded as the best kept secret in town. Don't expect anybody to tell you where that shelter is, if they will even admit that they know it exists!

THESE COLORS WON'T RUN

How did a fight over a painted masonry wall inadvertently produce one of Mount Dora's most unusual private homes?

One could argue that the painting *The Starry Night* by Dutch postimpressionist van Gogh shows up so frequently that art books and websites have become a little oversaturated. Still, with its blue vortex sky and shimmering moon and stars, it's hard to argue that looking upon it doesn't have a calming effect. This was certainly the case for the autistic son of Mount Dora residents Lubomir Jastrzebski and Nancy Nemhauser, who decided to commission artist Richard Barrenechea to put the iconic painting on what may be one of the very few places it had not previously appeared: the masonry wall around their house.

While their son found the resulting artwork tranquil and soothing, city officials found it far less so. So much less so, in fact, that they slapped the couple with a graffiti code violation and deemed the painting to be illegal signage. Despite somewhat flimsy reasoning, the city officials informed the couple that the masonry wall needed to match the house, thinking that would settle things and return the wall to its former and considerably more bland appearance.

Not wanting to run afoul of the law, the couple complied . . . but not quite how the city intended. Instead of painting over the masonry wall, they called the artist back in to make the exterior wall of their home into a more complete mural of the van Gogh painting.

Once you're done checking out the *Starry Night* house, you can explore the Modernism Museum, shop for local art and crafts at Under Cherry Blossom, or have food and drinks at the Goblin Market Restaurant & Lounge.

By this time, the local dustup had drawn national attention and overwhelming neighborhood support for the artwork (as demonstrated by more than 12,000 signatures on a change. org petition). In the face of this backlash, the city council voted unanimously to settle the issue and Mayor Nick Girone issued a public apology.

Today it's colorful paint rather than controversy swirling around this truly one-of-a-kind abode.

AN EARFUL OVER VAN GOGH

WHAT: The *Starry Night* house

WHERE: 401 W Old US Hwy. 441, Mount Dora

COST: Free

PRO TIP: Another nearby public art oddity is the *VW Bug Spider*. As of yet, no word on how city officials feel about that one.

The vibrantly painted exterior of the Starry Night *house. Photo by Joshua Ginsberg*

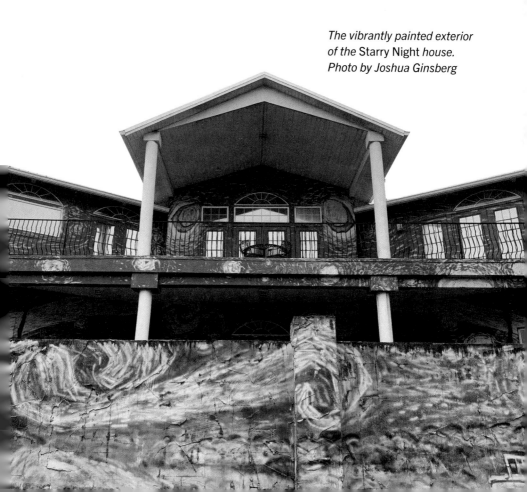

POWER, CORRUPTION, AND LIES

What's the scoop on the bronze bust recently installed in Mount Dora's Sunset Park?

To the small and exclusive club of female journalists recognized with public monuments, a new name was added in 2021: that of Mabel Norris Reese.

Reese arrived in Florida in 1947 when she bought a small weekly paper called the *Mount Dora Topic*, just two years before the infamous case of the "Groveland Four," in which four Black men were accused of raping a white Woman. Two of those men won a retrial in 1951, but when Sheriff Willis McCall went alone to pick them up, he shot them both along a dark stretch of road, sending one to the hospital and the other to the morgue. As Reese investigated the matter, the sheriff's claim of self-defense started to unravel. When she went public with this in an op-ed piece, the response was swift. Conflicts with Willis and the Ku Klux Klan escalated with her investigation into the case of Jesse Daniels, a mentally impaired teenager accused of rape.

INDELIBLE

WHAT: The Bust of Mabel Norris Reese

WHERE: Sunset Park, 230 W 4th Ave., Mount Dora

COST: Free

PRO TIP: If you want to learn more about Mabel Norris Reese, pick up a copy of Pulitzer Prize–winning author Gilbert King's book *Beneath a Ruthless Sun.*

Into his original terra-cotta version of the bust, sculptor Jim McNalis incorporated dirt from Reese's yard and the "M" and "R" keys from her typewriter.

Dead fish were dumped on her porch, she was threatened with violence, a cross was burned in her yard, her dog was poisoned, her office was vandalized, and her home was bombed. Twice.

Despite the risks she faced, Reese continued to be a voice for victims of injustice, including the Irish Indian Platt boys who were denied entrance to all-White public schools.

By 1958, however, the ongoing conflicts had taken a toll on Reese's business and personal life. She moved to Daytona Beach but continued her investigative work, earning 30 national newspaper awards including the Elijah Parish Lovejoy Award for Courage in Journalism, and a Pulitzer Prize nomination.

Reese's bust now stands firm, appropriately, in the very same city she was once driven from for unflinchingly exposing injustice and corruption.

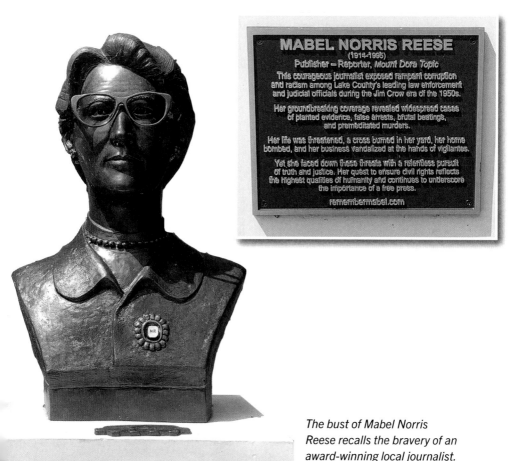

MABEL NORRIS REESE
(1914-1995)
Publisher – Reporter, *Mount Dora Topic*

This courageous journalist exposed rampant corruption and racism among Lake County's leading law enforcement and judicial officials during the Jim Crow era of the 1950s.

Her groundbreaking coverage revealed widespread cases of planted evidence, false arrests, brutal beatings, and premeditated murders.

Her life was threatened, a cross burned in her yard, her home bombed, and her business vandalized at the hands of vigilantes.

Yet she faced down these threats with a relentless pursuit of truth and justice. Her quest to ensure civil rights reflects the highest qualities of humanity and continues to underscore the importance of a free press.

remembermabel.com

The bust of Mabel Norris Reese recalls the bravery of an award-winning local journalist. Photo by Joshua Ginsberg

THE HOUSE THAT HATS BUILT

Why do cowboy hats, a magnificent mansion, and a university all share the same name?

One of the most famous and historic homes in the entire state of Florida sits in the quaint town of DeLand. It's called the Stetson Mansion, which lies just blocks away from the university that also shares the Stetson name. And although people might know the name of Stetson University, they may not realize that it is indeed the namesake for the world-famous hats as well.

The home was built for John B. Stetson, who is world famous for his hat company and is actually the man who invented the cowboy hat. Stetson rose to prominence in the 1860s during the era in which practically everyone wore a hat. His company was based in Philadelphia and one of the largest in the industry, so his wealth grew rapidly. His great riches allowed him to travel extensively and hobnob with other wealthy and powerful men. One of those men, Henry DeLand (yes, that DeLand), invited Stetson to visit the town (then named Persimmon Hollow) in the 1880s.

Needless to say, Stetson fell in love with the area. He had the home built in 1886 one year after his first visit and it became his "winter compound" until his death in 1906. The three-story home was exquisite, built with the highest level of quality that a man of his means could buy, all on a 300-acre orange farm. It consists

---

Henry DeLand came to Florida due to "Orange Fever." This is the made-up condition for people who were interested in buying land in Florida in the late 1800s. On his first trip, he purchased a large plot of land in what would later become the town named after him, DeLand.

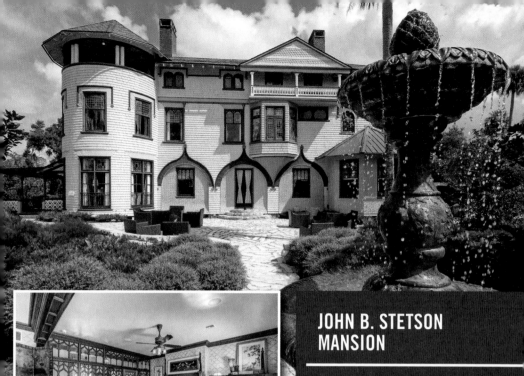

John B. Stetson built his marvelous mansion on the outskirts of DeLand after falling in love with the area. The home is now open for tours on select days. Photos courtesy of Stetson Mansion

JOHN B. STETSON MANSION

WHAT: The historical mansion owned by the founder of Stetson hats

WHERE: 1031 Camphor Ln., DeLand

COST: Adults are $34, youth are $22.

PRO TIP: Make a day of it. DeLand is a beautiful small town with a downtown shopping area worth exploring. The Athens Theatre puts on amazing performances and nearby restaurants like Cress win nationwide awards for excellence.

of over 10,000 square feet with gazebos, greenhouses, carriage rooms, gardens, and luxurious entertaining areas, and was one of the first homes in the world to be built with Edison electricity thanks to his close relationship with Thomas Edison. In 1978, the home was put on the US National Register of Historic Places.

POUNDING THE PAVEMENT

Why are Model Ts, tractor tires, and a movie theater connected?

There is a small theater in Winter Garden that is still operating today and packing the house with amazing performances. In fact, the Garden Theater still inhabits a building that was designed as a theater back in 1935. That early performing arts center thrived during World War II as residents would pack the theater to hear the latest from the war front along with the latest films. But the one thing it could not overcome in the 1960s was the exploding medium known as television. Once people were able to sit home and watch shows without venturing out, that spelled doom for the Garden Theater and many others like it around the country.

Next door to the theater was a bustling automobile business called Pounds Motor Company. Hoyle Pounds opened up the shop in the 1920s and set up what became the oldest "grove machinery" dealership in Florida. In addition to farm implements, he also sold Ford Model T cars, which is where two diverse worlds met. Tractors were great at driving across rugged, sandy roads. But the early model cars needed paved roads for their tires to work efficiently. When roads started being paved for cars, it caused a problem for tractors with metal wheels to drive across them. So, Pounds invented the first rubber tires for tractors at that small business to solve that problem and forever changed the industry, earning him the nickname "Mr. Tractor."

Here is where the theater and the dealership collide. When the theater closed, Pounds was expanding rapidly, so he bought the theater to house all the tires while he manufactured next door. Pounds was known as a tinkerer and was constantly looking for ways to improve machinery. He is credited with several other inventions, including

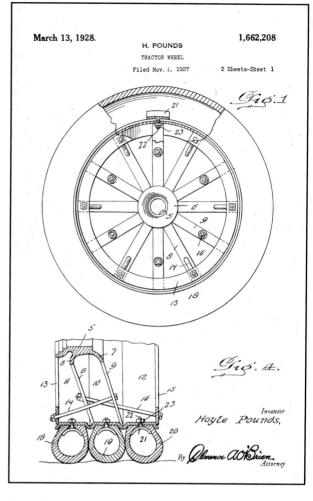

Hoyle Pounds invented the rubber tractor tire at his business in downtown Winter Garden. It was one of his many inventions.

the invention of a mowing deck, which he designed for a friend. That became the building block for Snapper lawn mowers.

Pounds Motor Company is long gone, but Hoyle's legacy lives on. The historical museums in Winter Garden give a greater understanding of how this small town played such a big part in Florida's history.

HISTORY IN THE HALLS

Why is one of the oldest hotels in Florida called "Edgewater," when it's not on the edge of any water?

A 1920s-era hotel in downtown Winter Garden has seen it all, from the ups, the downs, big-time celebrities . . . and giant fish. The Edgewater Hotel was first built to capitalize on the proximity to Lake Apopka, although it is about a mile from the water. But for people from up north who were looking for a fishing destination at the "largemouth bass capital of the world" in warm Florida, this was great marketing!

Fishermen (including Clark Gable) came from around the world to try their luck on the lake. But when the citrus industry dried up in the 1950s and '60s and the lake turned into a polluted mess, tourism stopped and the hotel, along with the city, fell into a downward spiral.

The historic building suffered through some tough times until new owners decided to restore it to its former glory as a bed-and-breakfast hotel. They refurbished the building and even restored one of the oldest operating elevators in the country. The Edgewater now sits in the middle of a town that is also going through a renaissance. Winter Garden has even been nicknamed a "modern-day Mayberry."

Another positive development for the town and the hotel is that the lake is being restored and fish and wildlife are returning in

The Edgewater Hotel still stands in downtown Winter Garden but isn't actually on the edge of water. But it was where celebrities and fishermen came when they wanted to fish Lake Apopka, the "largemouth bass capital of the world."

abundance. In fact, Lake Apopka held its first fishing tournament in decades as the nation emerged from the pandemic.

As the entire town goes through a new boom, the Edgewater Hotel takes you back in time as you feel like you're actually living in a time capsule. There is still an operating barber shop on the first floor, along with an ice cream parlor and a pair of restaurants.

EDGEWATER HOTEL

WHAT: Historic hotel in downtown Winter Garden

WHERE: 99 W Plant St., Winter Garden

COST: Rooms start at $124 a night.

PRO TIP: There are miles of trails nearby, so bring along your bicycle. You can also rent a bike at one of the bike shops near the hotel.

The West Orange Trail leads right to the front of the Edgewater Hotel. It is built on former railroad tracks and will eventually be connected to the 250-mile Coast-to-Coast Connector Trail.

A DEEP DIVE IN THE MIDDLE OF FLORIDA

Where can you scuba dive right in the middle of the state?

When most people think of diving in Florida, they likely think of the crystal-clear waters off the coast of the Keys. However, one of the most unusual underwater adventures lies inside of a prehistoric cave not far from Williston, right in the middle of the peninsula at Devil's Den.

First of all, the name: Devil's Den was given that name hundreds of years ago by early inhabitants who routinely saw the fog rising out of the ground-level opening of the cave on cool mornings. The underground spring is always 72 degrees, so it's cool in the summer and warm in the winter, which makes for a ghostly scene as you approach the natural wonder. The opening of the den has gradually widened over the years due to nature and man, so more sunlight now enters the abyss. But it still has an eerie appearance as vegetation surrounds the opening, giving it a true "underworld" feeling.

Even though the cave has been enjoyed by divers for the past few decades, the history of this ancient grotto goes way back in time. The remains of many extinct animals from the Pleistocene Age (2 million to 10,000 years ago) have been discovered at Devil's Den, along with the bones of early man dating back

PREHISTORIC PLUNGE

WHAT: Devil's Den

WHERE: 5390 NE 180th Ave., Williston

COST: Prices vary by which activity you choose.

PRO TIP: Why not make a weekend of it? Devil's Den also offers camping and cabins on-site. You don't need to bring the diving equipment as they rent everything you need.

Devil's Den near Ocala is a great place to snorkel or scuba dive in the crystal-clear waters of the grotto. Photo courtesy of Devil's Den

thousands of years. So this earthly attraction has long been a source of life, sustenance, and shelter in central Florida.

People enjoy the cave today by diving and snorkeling in the 54-foot-deep "inverted mushroom" diving area. You enter the cave via stairs and arrive at the diving platform where it takes a moment to take it all in. And if you don't know how to scuba dive, you can even train to get certified in the spring. Devil's Den is truly a natural wonder and a step back in time a short drive north of Orlando.

People are often surprised to learn that Florida has many caves because it's so flat. But the millions of years of buildup of coral and shells have made for amazing cave networks as the acidic waters washed away areas to be explored.

CALLING QUETZALCOATL

Did ancient Mesoamericans build a temple complex in central Florida?

How often have you thought to yourself, if only there was a place where I could spend a day exploring art and history museums, visiting working artists in their studios, catching a wedding reception, and learning the history of telephony and carpentry, all within a DIY Mayan Revival—styled compound? If you answered even once, you're in luck, because that specific and uniquely improbable combination is known locally as the Art & History Museums Maitland (A&H for short).

The story begins with artist-architect Jules Andre Smith, who established his "Research Studio" for experimental art in 1937, which was composed of twelve buildings on 2.84 acres of land and financed largely by Mary Curtis Bok. These buildings became home to a colony of many nationally recognized artists such as Milton Avery, Doris Lee, and others. Today it's known as the Maitland Art Center and the largest of A&H's museums.

Founded in 1970, the Maitland Historical Society began compiling a trove of artifacts and information, which led to the creation of three more museums as part of the complex, including the Telephone Museum in 1982, the Waterhouse Residence Museum in 1992, and the Carpentry Shop Museum in 1994.

Connecting all of the various museums and buildings are picturesque gardens, muraled and tiled walkways, and buildings that appear to have been transported through time and space from ancient Mesoamerica.

Want to see authentic Incan, Mayan, and Peruvian art and artifacts? Inside the Orlando Museum of Art you'll find their world-class Art of the Ancient Americas Collection.

MY OH MAYAN

WHAT: Art & History Museums Maitland

WHERE: 231 W Packwood Ave., Maitland

COST: General admission to the main campus museums is $6; seniors, children, and Maitland residents get in for $5; and just $4 covers Maitland seniors/children as well as military personnel.

PRO TIP: If you visit on a weekend, there's a good chance that a wedding or other event will be in progress. Try not to photobomb someone's special day, and hands off the cake.

A walk through the buildings and grounds of the Art & History Museums Maitland would surely impress any ancient Mesoamerican deity. Photo by Joshua Ginsberg

As one of the few remaining examples of Mayan Revival architecture in the southeastern United States, the Maitland Art Center was designated a historic landmark. It is also available as a venue for weddings and other events, so if you're looking for a truly one-of-a-kind setting to tie the knot, throw a cocktail party, or make a sacrificial offering to the Mayan serpent god Kukulcan (please don't), this might be the ideal place.

ONCE UPON A TIME IN MAITLAND

Where's the most unique place in central Florida to see the stars?

When the Tiedtke family opened the Enzian Theater in Maitland in 1985, it was the beginning of a beautiful friendship. For its first four years it operated as a repertory house showing up to a dozen classic films each week and sharing the spotlight with a variety of artists and musicians (not least of which was composer Philip Glass).

In 1989, the Enzian decided to focus on being more of an alternative art-house venue showing first-run independent features, which was risky business at the time. Their gamble paid off and made the Enzian a rising star on the cultural scene, bright enough to draw national attention. In 1991 they began hosting the Florida Film Festival, which is the only Oscar-qualifying film festival in the state. It might not be quite as well known or star-studded as Cannes and Sundance, but Christopher Walken, Susan Sarandon, and Giancarlo Esposito are just a few of the A-listers known to make an appearance there.

In 2008, the Enzian added the Eden Bar—a 2,000-square-foot outdoor eatery surrounded by massive oaks, a fountain, and

ROLL CREDITS

WHAT: The Enzian Theater and Eden Bar

WHERE: 1300 Orlando Ave., Maitland

COST: Regular ticket pricing $12.50, student/senior/military (with ID) $11, matinees $11, film society members $10

PRO TIP: The Florida Film Festival is not the theater's only event. Also worth checking out is the Reel Short Teen Film Festival, Kidfest, South Asian Film Festival, Jewish Film Festival, and the Brouhaha film and video showcase.

A visit to the Enzian is a must for any lover of independent films and theaters.
Photo by Joshua Ginsberg

a gorgeous courtyard, which has become the neighborhood's go-to spot for date night and brunch. Today the Enzian continues to show alternative, foreign, and self-distributed films on their single screen and describes itself as central Florida's only full-time, nonprofit independent theater.

The theater's least known feature is probably its resident scream queen—the ghost of a disembodied, screaming woman's head said to make rare cameo appearances on moonless nights around 1 a.m. She begins in the north corner of the theater, floats around the room shrieking, then disappears through the wall. Who she is and what she wants with the living is unknown. Some have suggested that she's unhappy with the choice of films. Everybody's a critic, right?

Talon show: Just down the street from the Enzian is the Audubon Center for Birds of Prey, which offers an opportunity to view kites, owls, bald eagles, falcons, and ospreys.

DEATH IN ALTAMONTE SPRINGS

What is the most surprising innovation to have come out of Altamonte Springs?

Less than 20 minutes north of Orlando, with a population of around 50,000 people, the city of Altamonte Springs seems like any other cute little central Florida suburban oasis, a pleasant place to settle down and raise a family that you can take to Cranes Roost Park on the weekends for the choreographed fountain show. The city website touts it as being "born of innovation, fiscal responsibility, and progressive ideas," but somehow, for all that, they left out what may be this burb's most unique claim to fame—as home to one of the first true death metal bands.

For those unfamiliar with this extreme subgenre of heavy metal, it evolved from bands like Slayer, Megadeth, and Anthrax, except it was louder, heavier, less intelligible, lyrically darker, and more morbid, delivered in growls and snarls, and just all around more intense in every conceivable way. Precisely the way that Chuck Schuldiner, Kam Lee, and Rick Rozz liked it when they came together in 1984 and formed the band Mantas.

Influenced by kindred sonic pioneers like Possessed and Necrophagia, the band released several rehearsal tapes and their *Death by Metal* demo before reforming under the name

Altamonte Springs is also home to the self-proclaimed world's largest nativity scene and a somewhat creepy visage of Jesus carved in such a way that his gaze seems to follow you. No doubt he's there to keep watch on all that local "devil music."

The suburban family home and garage where some of the very first death metal was ever played. Photo by Joshua Ginsberg

for which they are best known, Death, and releasing a second demo titled *Reign of Terror*.

The location and lineup of band members changed, but by 1986 Schuldiner was back in Orlando and working with drummer Chris Reifert on their first full release, *Scream Bloody Gore*, which became a model for the nascent form of heavy metal. The band went on to produce seven studio albums and another ten live albums before Schuldiner succumbed to pneumonia following treatment for a brain tumor in 2001, after which the band dispersed.

Today, though not advertised, you can still find the home where Schuldiner plucked his first guitar chords.

ROCK SPRINGS REVISITED

Where is the "original" lazy river in Orlando?

One of the most pristine lazy rivers to float down in an inner tube is not at a local water park. No, the Rock Springs Run at Kelly Park is not only one of the prettiest floats in central Florida, it is also one of the oldest! The main problem here according to locals in the Apopka area is that it used to be a hidden gem, but now it's so popular that you often have to be in line hours before the park opens if you want to get in, especially during the summer when school is out.

The 68-degree spring is just one part of Kelly Park but is certainly the reason swimmers flock here. When you arrive at the park and see the water, you don't really get an understanding of how great this park is. In order to ride the river, you have to walk about a half mile through the woods on a paved path to the actual spring itself. That is where you put in your inflatable device and experience the entire "run." It takes about 20 minutes to make the whole run, then a short walk back to the start. You can also rent tubes

THE ORIGINAL PREHISTORIC LAZY RIVER

WHAT: Kelly Park/Rock Springs

WHERE: 400 E Kelly Park Rd., Apopka

COST: $3 per vehicle for 1–2 people, $5 per vehicle for 3–8 people, and $1 for additional person/walk-ins/motorcycles/bikes.

PRO TIP: During the week, arrive about an hour before the park opens. On weekends, make it a couple hours of sitting in your car before the park opens.

Bonus Tip: Bring along the snorkel gear.

A natural lazy river flows from a massive spring at Kelly Park. The clear, cold waters of the Rock Springs are a nice refresher on hot Florida afternoons.
Photo by Sophia Brown

near the park if you forgot or simply don't want to haul the extra baggage to the park.

You will see some people scooping up handfuls of sand and shells. But what they are really looking for are those rare shark teeth that occasionally surface in the area. There are also plenty of beaches to hang out on if you don't feel like chasing the kids up paths.

WALT DISNEY ON ICE

Is the famed entertainment mogul actually cryogenically frozen below his own amusement park?

Ask any 12-year-old what they know about Walt Disney and you'll probably get two different answers. One is that he created the Disney entertainment empire, with its massive theme parks based on the animation studio where Mickey Mouse and a great many other animated characters were brought to life.

The other response you might hear is the urban legend that Walt himself is also waiting to be brought to life at some future point via the miracles of cryogenics. Most versions of the myth allege that his frozen body is located either under the Pirates of the Caribbean ride in Disneyland or in a specially designed chamber within the labyrinth of tunnels below Disney World.

The legend apparently started circulating shortly after Walt's death in December of 1966 from complications of lung cancer, following which he was cremated and interred at Forest Lawn Memorial Park in Glendale, California (unless, as some suggest, that was all merely staged). The rumor appeared in print for the first time in a 1969 *Ici Paris* article in which an executive posited that it came from the studio artists trying to have the last laugh over their erstwhile boss. If so, it seems they succeeded and the legend has taken root, fueled by Walt's well-documented fixations on seeing the future and maintaining his privacy.

Over time the myth has been kept alive by mischievous trainers, who are said to occasionally whisper to new hires as they pass

---

Disney World's tunnels are designed to be nearly invisible, but the abandoned Discovery Island in Bay Lake sits in plain sight. That is not an invitation to try and discover it for yourself, unless you're looking to get Disney banned.

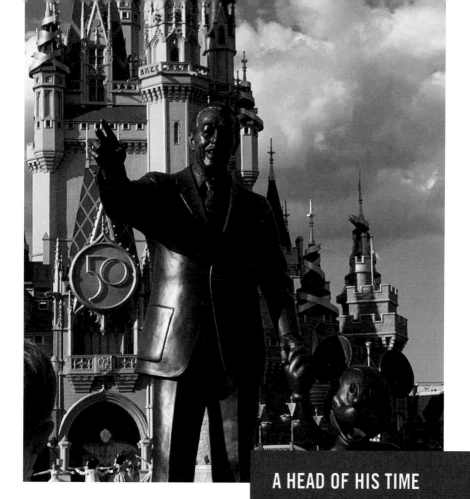

You can find this statue of Walt (with head firmly attached to body) in front of Cinderella Castle. Photo by Joshua Ginsberg

A HEAD OF HIS TIME

WHAT: Walt Disney's frozen body

WHERE: Not under Disney World—it's just a myth

COST: The Keys to the Kingdom Tour takes guests into the tunnels as part of a five-hour walking tour for $99.

PRO TIP: "Fantasy and reality often overlap." —Walt Disney

through the tunnel system under Disney World, "We don't go that way—it leads to Walt's chamber." In 2018, Benjamin Lancaster also released a guerrilla-style comedy titled *The Further Adventures of Walt's Frozen Head*, thus ensuring that the tale of Walt's preservation will endure alongside Peter Pan and Snow White as a fairy tale for generations to come.

A VIEW FROM THE TOP

Is there really a room in Cinderella's Castle where only VIPs get to stay?

This is truly a Disney secret hidden in plain sight. This used to be a much bigger secret, but word has gotten out about the amazing room high in the castle overlooking Disney World. Only a few select guests have ever been allowed to stay in the suite that looks like a French château and many of those guests don't seem to want to talk publicly about their stay. Thankfully, the folks at Disney were kind enough to finally allow the media into the suite so the world could see what was hidden.

If you look at the castle from Fantasyland, you will see three stained glass windows high on the castle. Those are the windows that hide one of the most secretive parts of the park. The floor is adorned with intricate mosaics, and a large fireplace gives just the right ambiance. The master bedroom is just what you would

THE CINDERELLA CASTLE SUITE

WHAT: Luxury suite high in Cinderella's Castle

WHERE: Walt Disney World's Magic Kingdom

COST: Don't even try!

PRO TIP: There are dozens of secrets hidden all around Disney World. If you get a chance, spend a day searching for the hidden Mickeys and other secret locations in the parks.

This suite was built as a place for Walt Disney to stay, but he died before the park was completed. There is also a hidden airplane runway near the entrance to the park where Walt used to land his plane. That can still be seen from satellite images just east of the roadway as you approach the park.

The calm before the crowds. A rare glimpse of no crowds on Main Street USA at Walt Disney World with Cinderella Castle in the distance. Photo by John Brown

expect in a royal castle with four-poster beds ornately draped with curtains. The bathroom has a massive, jetted tub that is surrounded by three mosaic masterpieces on the three walls. Above the fireplace is a mirror that magically turns into a television.

And if you are wondering about the price, keep wondering. Since it's only for VIPs or prize winners, there likely isn't a cost at all, so we will never know what it costs to live like a princess at Disney. And to make sure you never forget your magical experience, you even get to take home a glass slipper at the end of your stay.

X MARKS THE SPOT

Did Walt Disney really draw an X on the map for where Disney World would be built?

You have probably seen the image by now of Walt Disney standing next to a map of central Florida with a giant X symbolizing where he was going to build his theme park. So from that angle, yes, he did draw an X on the map. But this story has so many secrets and twists and turns that it's much deeper than that. That fact of the matter is he first spotted the location while flying over the swampland while leaving Florida.

The story dates to 1963 when Walt was looking for ways to expand his theme parks. He had just had a meeting in St. Louis to build a park along the Mississippi River where the Gateway Arch would soon stand. He had also met with city leaders in Niagara Falls. Even though there was some promise with those sites, he wanted a climate where tourists could enjoy the park year-round and where there was less competition for entertainment dollars.

Disney came to Florida in November to check out sites near West Palm Beach, Ocala, and Tampa. He realized he didn't want the park near the beach because that was free competition! As he was heading back to California he flew over the area of Florida's Turnpike and Interstate 4 where he saw thousands of acres of empty land. As he looked out the window of the jet, he said,

---

Walt Disney's flight on November 21, 1963, also has a story. He was headed back home to California but had to stop in New Orleans for fuel. When he landed, he was informed by the crews at the airport that President John F. Kennedy had been shot. The future of Walt Disney World was set on the same day Kennedy was assassinated.

Walt Disney was a master at studying human behavior and traffic patterns. When he saw the convergence of highways near Orlando from his airplane, he knew where the theme parks needed to be built.

THE DISNEY COLLECTION

WHAT: Collection of rarely seen Disney documents and memorabilia

WHERE: Orlando Public Library, 101 E Central Blvd.

COST: Free to enter

PRO TIP: Visit the library before your next trip to Disney. It will give a better understanding of the history of the park, along with historical nuggets that you can't find anywhere else.

"That's it." That 12,400 acres was owned by the Demetree family, who eventually sold it to Disney. His team also started buying up land under different names so as not to arouse suspicion.

All of these stories, along with Walt's personal notes and press clippings, can be found in an amazing collection of Disney artifacts at the Orlando Public Library. Disney fans from around the world have visited to learn little-known facts about Walt and the parks.

IT TAKES A VILLAGES

Does one family own the fastest-growing town in America?

The sprawling retirement community north of Orlando straddling Sumter, Lake, and Marion Counties has gone from "Florida's Friendliest Hometown" into the fastest-growing metro area in the country in just a few short years. It basically started out as mail-order land tracts sold by Harold Schwartz and another partner until that practice was outlawed in 1968. A 400-lot mobile home park called Orange Blossom Gardens was later developed on a small part of the land that was purchased by Schwartz along with his son H. Gary Morse. But they were still struggling selling lots in the years that followed.

It was Morse who convinced his father that they needed to develop something unique if they were ever to sell the land. That's when they decided to make the property like a "dream come true" for retirees who were looking for a small-town feel and plenty of activities along with the Florida lifestyle. And by 1992, the Villages had been born.

Although most people assume the Villages is a town, it is actually a large master-planned community. The area is still unincorporated and is comprised of around 80 villages, each with its own name and unique characteristics. Morse gave the ownership of the Villages to his children in 2006 and stayed behind the scenes until his death in 2014.

So, what's next for this amazing little village? More growth. What used to be a secret piece of Florida paradise has become

THE VILLAGES

WHAT: "Florida's Friendliest Hometown"

WHERE: Spanish Springs Town Square, 1120 Main St., The Villages

COST: It costs nothing to drive around and see why people are flocking there.

PRO TIP: When visiting, rent a golf cart. There is no better way to experience the community than driving around in some of the custom-made carts.

Golf carts going across one of the Villages bridges. The Villages has become one of the fastest-growing master-planned communities in the country. Photo courtesy of Sophia Brown

the worst-kept secret in the country. The population in the metro area around the Villages was estimated at 139,900 in 2022. The population is expected to be more than 452,000 in 2060. That is a 223 percent increase and the highest of any city in the United States. And it's still family owned!

Golf is king in the Villages. There are currently 711 holes of golf on more than 50 courses. This makes it the single largest golf community in the world.

A HIDDEN GEM AMONG THE BRICKS

Why is a famous nature preserve located inside a theme park?

You may see the name LEGOLAND and say, what's so secret about that? Everyone knows about the wonderful theme park for little thrill seekers. But it's what's still "inside" LEGOLAND that is a secret in plain sight. Long before the kids park was even a thought, Cypress Gardens was a quintessential "Old Florida" attraction. It was such a gem that the image that many people had of central Florida in the 1950s and '60s was because of this park. Celebrities like Elvis and Johnny Carson made trips to the place where movies like *Easy to Love* and *Moon over Miami* were filmed on location.

Cypress Gardens was likely the backdrop for a postcard you saw as a child with daredevil water-skiers doing amazing tricks with enormous cypress trees in the background. The water-ski shows are still here, albeit with LEGO characters now on the water, as are the trees! One particular banyan tree that was planted in 1939 is still a centerpiece of the botanical gardens and it now has a limb-spread the size of an entire city block.

Of course, LEGOLAND Florida is worth the trip with the family. If you have kids under the age of 12, this may become your favorite park because everything is just their size. But the

There are many beautiful places in Florida, but this is one of the top. Why else would this be the filming location for so many movies and TV shows? *Sea Hunt*, *Easy to Love*, and *Moon over Miami* are just a few that used the setting in the films.

developers were wise enough to keep the nature preserve intact so that the adults have the added bonus of seeing spectacular Florida scenery. And that may be the biggest secret. Even though you will have to pull the kids away from the rides, you may be shocked at how much they love seeing Florida the way it used to be.

LEGOLAND AND CYPRESS GARDENS

WHAT: A beautiful nature preserve inside a theme park for children

WHERE: 1 LEGOLAND Way, Winter Haven

COST: General admission is $99 for a one-day ticket, but prices vary by time of year.

PRO TIP: Before you go, watch old videos on the internet about Cypress Gardens. This will give you a much better sense of the history of this park. One great movie in particular is *Cypress Gardens: 70 Years of Magic.*

Iconic images of the water-ski shows at Cypress Gardens. The shows still take place at LEGOLAND.

GHOUL'S NIGHT OUT

Is there a place in town to scare up a stiff drink?

"Sometimes you want to go / where everybody makes you scream / and it's always Halloween . . ."

Wait a minute, that's not how the lyrics go to the opening of an episode of *Cheers* . . . but it could very well be the start of a theme song for Cocktails and Screams—a horror-themed bar in downtown Orlando. For those who enjoy their spirits in the company of spirits, it is an experience not to be missed.

The bar was opened in October of 2019 by the same owners of the arcade bar Joysticks, in a space alleged to have once provided overflow capacity for carpenter and embalmer Elijah Hand. Today visitors might be greeted by a cast of creepy characters (such as Jack Skellington, Beetlejuice, and others). Inside there's a wall of vintage masks, horror posters galore, a stage with a pipe organ, VIP "crypts" (in both the *Munsters* and *Addams Family* styles) and a re-created hallway from the Overlook Hotel. There's also a display case of authentic and replica movie props such as the Hellraiser puzzle box, a *Teen Wolf* varsity jacket, the orb from *Phantasm*, and dozens of other iconic objects.

IT'S A DEAD MAN'S PARTY

WHAT: Cocktails and Screams

WHERE: 39 W Pine St.

COST: Most of their signature drinks are between $14 and $16.

PRO TIP: Remember to tip your server—failure to do so is poor form and may or may not land you with a hex.

The bar, which resembles the lab of a mad scientist, serves up spine-tingling concoctions including the Bone Daddy, Hocus Pocus, Donnie Darko, Uncle Fester, Supernatural, and other tasty elixirs.

Hidden within the bar is also a second, speakeasy-styled room known as the Craft, available to those who can find it. Once inside, scare meets flair in what resembles the hut of a voodoo

Flair meets scare inside the bar's spooky speakeasy known as the Craft.
Photo by Joshua Ginsberg

witch doctor or priestess. Rather than a menu, guests are given the option of either a tincture (single) or a potion (double), which is then custom made based on each patron's preferences, along with occasional fire breathing, bottle twirling, and ice carving.

If you're impressed enough to want to take home some merch, stop by the boo-tique counter before you leave.

Bar None Creations, which operates Cocktails and Screams, has other pop-up and permanent themed bars including the arcade-styled 1Up Orlando and Wonderland-inspired High-T.

ON THE CUTTING EDGE

What brand of knife was designed for and carried into space by all Mercury Seven astronauts?

It's a common lament among those of previous generations that the quality of American-made products just isn't what it used to be. The folks at Randall Made Knives, however, are keen to disagree on that point. The family business, now in its third generation, still follows a 17-step process, which allows them to produce about 8,000 of their extremely sought-after knives each year. Randall Made Knives' quality, following, and wait list (of six years or more) makes owning one akin to having a small Harley-Davidson in a sheath.

Visitors can get a closer look at the Randall collection inside what was the former estate home on the property. There you'll find one of the largest private collections of pocketknives, a giant switchblade and Swiss Army knife, and a staggering variety of swords, stilettos, machetes, knives, axes, pikes, and anything else with a sharp metal edge.

Throughout the 4,000-square-foot company museum, between its rows and racks of deadly weapons, you'll learn the story of Bo Randall, who founded the company in 1938, and read testimonials from hunters, generals, presidents, and celebrities. In fact, it wouldn't be hyperbole to say that Randall Knives are "out of this world," as NASA approached the company in the early 1960s to design a survival knife for its astronauts. The resulting Model 17 "Astro" was issued to all of the Mercury

If axes are your edged weapon of choice, you can practice throwing them at Rockstar Axe Throwing, Epic Axe Throwing, BATL Axe Throwing, Stumpy's Hatchet House, and at least a half dozen other locations nearby.

GET TO THE POINT

WHAT: Randall Knife Museum

WHERE: 4857 S Orange Blossom Trl.

COST: Free

PRO TIP: The museum is open Monday through Thursday from 10 a.m. to 4 p.m. Look for a small sign along South Orange Blossom Trail.

An extraordinary collection of edged weapons now occupies the first floor of what was once a private home. Photos by Joshua Ginsberg

Seven astronauts and carried by Gordon Cooper when he made his orbit of Earth in 1963, making it the first fixed-blade knife in space.

While the "Astro" models are a rare find for collectors, the Model 3 "Hunter," Model 9 "Pro-Thrower," and the Model 26 "Pathfinder" will be easier to acquire.

CURIOUS GOODS

Where can you find the ideal contents for your Victorian *wunderkammer*?

Surely it's a problem you've had before: you've been invited to a friend's sabbat or a secret society initiation, but you're not sure which hooded cloak to wear and what to bring for your host. Fear not, there's more than one place in town to procure the perfect offering and attire for any occasion or ritual.

Prometheus Esoterica is a logical first stop for those uncommon items on your shopping list. From gothic decor and artwork to funerary items, surgical devices, vampire-hunting kits, ornately carved bones and skulls, tarot decks, even an occasional authentic shrunken human head, here you'll find essentially anything that might be missing from Baba Yaga's pantry or a coven's broom closet. Owned by husband and wife Whitney Hayes and Adam DeLancett, the store expanded in 2019 from the back of an antique shop to open its own crypt of curiosities and a café with flavored coffees from Clermont-based Coffee Shop of Horrors, many of which pack enough caffeine to wake the dead. While you're there, don't miss "Ostrich Hepburn"—she's the one with the long neck wearing a tiara.

If you stop by Prometheus Esoterica around yuletide, you might be able to get your family holiday photos posing with a goat-headed Krampus. Photos by Joshua Ginsberg

If your taste in collectibles is more scientific than occult, Darwin & Wallace has a selection of diaphanized specimens, fossils, and taxidermy that would make Robert Ripley envious. Their selection runs from the fairly accessible like trilobites, shark teeth, plant fossils, and cephalopod cast replicas to prized rarities such as allosaurus vertebrae, two-headed calf skulls, and the like. They also do custom projects, so if you were thinking of turning that stash of phalanges into a necklace or making a crown out of squid beaks, these are the folks to talk to.

Even if you're disturbed by what you find on display, you can rest in peace knowing that it's all been sourced legally and ethically.

Other local purveyors of metaphysical goods include Avalon, A Spiral Circle, and Shifting Souls. Even the Wizarding World of Harry Potter inside Universal Studios Florida offers a darker shopping experience in Knockturn Alley.

DEEP CANYONS IN A FLAT STATE

Why are there massive canyons in the middle of the woods in Marion County?

Orlando is known as the theme park capital of the world. That is certainly not a secret. But if you want to enjoy one of the most thrilling rides in the country, you only have to venture back into the woods near Ocala into an area that looks nothing like Florida should look. And the only way to see this bizarre land feature is via a zip line.

The oddity is a combination of old-growth forests, massive canyons, and pristine blue waters. The canyons are actually old limestone quarries that were carved out of the hard Florida ground and have now filled in with beautiful turquoise water that looks more like Jamaica than Ocala. Mining of the limestone stopped back in the 1930s and the area has been practically untouched since then. And quite frankly, very few people even saw these beautiful geographical wonders until recently. And that's where the zip line comes in.

The Canyons Zip Line and Adventure Park was built for a bit of adventure and Florida history all rolled into one. The numerous zip lines are billed as "Florida's highest, longest, and

THE CANYONS ZIP LINE AND CANOPY TOURS

WHAT: Adventure and zip line park

WHERE: 8045 NW Gainesville Rd., Ocala

COST: The Sky High tour is $55.99. The ultimate Big Cliff Canyon is $109.99.

PRO TIP: If you are really brave, one of the best tours happens at dark when the moon is full. You get to fly through the air with only the light of the full moon to light the way as you glide across the treetops with the canyons below.

The quarries left behind after mining operations near Ocala are some of the most picturesque areas in the state. The zip line tours give you a unique perspective of the topography. Photo courtesy of the Canyons Zip Line

fastest zips." The 12 zip lines give you a bird's-eye view of the entire area. But if you aren't up for speedy thrills, you can also see the area via horseback and kayak.

Ocala is known as the "Horse Capital of the World" due to the amazing number of racehorses trained there and equestrian facilities in the area. The World Equestrian Center recently opened near Ocala and is now the largest equestrian complex in the United States.

BRITISH INVASION

Why does Orlando have such a British vibe in places?

There are dozens of British-themed bars and pubs across Orlando, which are not just tourist novelties but actually authentic locales, but that is only a part of this story. In fact, the history of Orlando is very connected to Great Britain, although most may not realize it. The history between the two goes back more than 100 years and also helps explain some of the names you see and hear daily.

The influx of British citizens to Orange County began in earnest in the 1880s when Florida began to run ads in Britain offering land for "a dollar an acre" in a location where they could make a good living. That appealed to many British families who packed up and moved to central Florida, with many of them settling in the areas near the Butler Chain of Lakes. One man purchased substantial land in the area and named it Windermere, after a lake by the same name in England. Two other men named their land Isleworth, named after the town near London. That land was later developed into the famous Isleworth Country Club.

And there is the historic Rogers Building in downtown Orlando, which happens to be one of the oldest buildings in Orlando that is still standing. It has transitioned over the years, but was initially called the English Club and was built to be an English gentlemen's club back in the 1880s.

Because of the large British influence in Orlando, the British Bonfire Night, or Guy Fawkes Day, is a big deal. It takes place on November 8 in Kissimmee and was started by the British American Chamber of Commerce. It is now known as one of the biggest celebrations of its type in the US.

The historical Wintermere Town Hall still sits in the middle of the city. The area was popular with early British families looking to move to Florida. Photo by John Brown

Even today, the influence of England is seen all over the area. A private establishment called London House brings a little bit of Great Britain to Sand Lake Road for members. There are even a few stores to immerse yourself in the culture, including the British Shoppe in Longwood and the British Isle Connection in Kissimmee.

BRITISH STORES AROUND ORLANDO

WHAT: British Shoppe

WHERE: 708 S US Hwy 17-92, Longwood

COST: Prices vary

PRO TIP: The British pubs around Orlando are always a good time. But you can elevate the experience if you time your visit with a soccer match featuring teams like Arsenal FC, Manchester City FC, or Chelsea FC.

THE BRIDGE TO NOWHERE

Why is there a bridge over the Wekiva River that leads to a dead end?

One of the most popular "hidden" hangouts in the Orlando area is an island in the middle of the Wekiva River. Wekiva Island is the name of the destination with a bar, a restaurant, an art gallery, a boardwalk, and so much more. But there is a secret that is hidden in plain sight right next to the popular establishment. It's a bridge to nowhere about which most people probably never stop and ponder, "Why did they build that?"

The bridge at the end of Miami Springs Drive in Longwood connects Seminole County to Orange County a little north of Wekiva Springs State Park. According to transportation officials, a highway was being designed that would connect Seminole, Orange, and Lake Counties by cutting across a forested area now called Wekiva Springs State Park. Their plans, however, were halted due to environmental concerns. But a private group had already built the bridge over the Wekiva River because they owned land along the corridor that they believed would be more valuable if the road was completed. So when the highway was stopped, they simply abandoned the bridge. And here is the next oddity: nobody really knows who owns the bridge so it's

---

The Wekiva River basin is a national treasure. It was designated as a "Wild and Scenic River" in 2000 and is now federally protected. The river is fed primarily by the Wekiwa Spring Run and the Rock Spring Run, both of which can be accessed by canoe since the river flows at a leisurely pace.

The "Bridge to Nowhere" near Wekiva Island. The road was supposed to connect Orange County to Lake County but was stopped to protect the Wekiva River basin. Photo by Sophia Brown

WEKIVA ISLAND

WHAT: An island getaway in the middle of central Florida

WHERE: 1014 Miami Springs Dr., Longwood

COST: $2 per person entrance fee. Activities cost extra.

PRO TIP: Rent a canopy for the day to experience the island life near this "secret." It's a place to get away from the sun and claim a comfy chair right next to the beautiful stream.

impossible to determine if it should be torn down or turned into some sort of attraction over the river.

So for now, it remains a part of the landscape just a stone's throw away from Wekiva Island. The good news is you can still see a piece of Florida history by renting a canoe or kayak nearby and floating under the true oddity. And you can also check out the art gallery on the island where proceeds from some of the artworks now protect the area through the Wekiva Wilderness Trust.

FESTIVE-SOUNDING FORTRESS

Why is there a fort in Florida named Christmas?

Not only is Fort Christmas named after one of our biggest holidays, but the nearby town also adopted the name after its historic founding. The name dates back to the day that US Army soldiers and Alabama volunteers arrived in the area west of Orlando on December 25, 1837. The soldiers had pushed into the area during the Second Seminole Indian War and began construction on the heavily guarded facility.

Those early days of war in the immediate area have now turned into a tranquil park that allows plenty of time and space for recreation and reflection. The original fort is now gone, but the full-size replica gives you a true understanding of the area's history and challenges.

The park and surrounding area also honor the name by hosting an amazing Christmas celebration as people from around the country flock to the town for Christmas card pictures. The Fort Christmas Cracker Christmas event is one of those nostalgic ways to get in the mood for

FORT CHRISTMAS HISTORICAL PARK

WHAT: Historic fort east of Orlando

WHERE: 1300 N Fort Christmas Rd., Christmas

COST: Free

PRO TIP: Bring along the Christmas cards. The post office sets up a booth so you can get a "Fort Christmas" stamp on all your letters.

There is a time capsule that was built into the fort when it was reconstructed in 1977. The capsule is set to be opened sometime in 2027.

The historic homes at Fort Christmas give insight into how families once lived in Florida. The nearby "working" post office is where many people mail their Christmas letters. Photos by Sophia Brown

CHRISTMAS
POST OFFICE

the holiday season. Cracker, by the way, refers to the sound made by the whips of early ranchers. The pioneer way of life is on full display during the holidays as you take a step back in time to how Florida was in the 1800s. What better place to celebrate Christmas than at Fort Christmas with the Spanish moss swaying in the breeze.

HAVE SPACE SUIT, WILL DONATE

Where can visitors get a more "down-to-earth" look at space exploration?

For some, the phrase "Space Coast" means specifically the Kennedy Space Center, which offers rocket launch viewings, films, interactive displays, and more. Unbeknownst to many though, less than a half hour away from Cape Canaveral is a far more personal gateway to the galaxy.

Rewind to the late 1990s when a local dentist visited Los Angeles and came back with stars in his eyes. He had been so impressed with the Hollywood Walk of Fame that he thought Titusville should have something similar to honor its space workers. He joined with others and their efforts resulted in the Space Walk of Fame inside Space View Park, with the handprints from 30 different off-world pioneers and monuments to the Apollo, Mercury, Gemini, and Space Shuttle programs.

When space workers began arriving to add their names to the monuments, they brought with them extraordinary pieces of space history for consignment and donation (ranging from mission pins and awards to launch manuals, rare photos, and actual items taken into space). By 2001 so many items had been donated that the organization needed a place to house its space reliquary. The museum moved a half dozen times before landing at its current site, where new artifacts are continually brought into its orbit, including scale models, computer terminals, space suits, and parts of spacecraft.

The museum now owns thousands of objects, roughly 500 of which are usually on display. Separate rooms are dedicated to women in the space program and to all those who toil tirelessly

Pull up a seat in front of original flight control monitors. Photo by Joshua Ginsberg

THE FINAL FRONTIER

WHAT: The American Space Museum and Walk of Fame

WHERE: 308 Pine St., Titusville

COST: Adults $10; seniors and military $8; teens $5; kids 12 and under are free.

PRO TIP: The museum's greatest asset is unquestionably its docents and staff, most of whom worked in the space program. Leave plenty of time, as their deep-dive guided tours can last for hours.

behind the scenes enabling humanity to reach the stars.

As a nonprofit organization, the museum relies on donations to stay aloft. Maybe the next time Jeff Bezos or Elon Musk are in town for a launch, they'll drop by and see as much value in preserving as in making space history.

At 4 p.m. Eastern most weekdays you can catch new episodes of the American Space Museum's "Stay Curious" broadcast on both YouTube and Facebook.

SPACE TO ROAM

Why did NASA pick Merritt Island as the place to launch rockets?

One of the most incredible things about being in central Florida is seeing a rocket launch from Cape Canaveral. It used to be a rare occurrence, but now it is becoming a weekly occurrence thanks to private launches. Even though it is a beautiful location for the launch sites, the location of Kennedy Space Center was not chosen by accident, but rather based on a lot of math and science.

In 1961, NASA began the purchase of land on Merritt Island on which to base the Apollo lunar landing program. One of the main criteria was being as south and east as possible. The rockets needed to be launched from the eastern United States because of the massive size of the booster rockets that needed to drop into the ocean, rather than somewhere over the continental United States. The southern criteria was also needed due to the earth's rotation. This is where the math comes in; the closer the launch is to the equator, the more linear velocity is available to jettison the rocket into orbit. Thus, Florida was perfect.

There is one other theory about the reason for the site selection, which deals with climatology. It has long been claimed that NASA chose the site because it is so difficult for a hurricane to hit that area of Florida. It is true that the Gulf Stream lies

Cape Canaveral has been the scene for many historical launches. After several years of a lull in launches, private space companies have now joined the Space Race and launches happen much more often.

about 30 miles off the coast of Brevard County and has the ability to weaken hurricanes, or even guide the storms away from the Space Coast. That may be an added benefit as no hurricane stronger than Category 3 has hit Brevard County since 1850. Even though that is a valuable asset, it appears to be more of a local legend than an actual deciding factor for NASA.

The nearby University of Central Florida was developed to train workers in the space industry. Most of the streets on campus have astrological names and the original mascot was the Citronaut, which is a combination of an orange and an astronaut.

I'VE A FEELING WE'RE NOT IN CAPE CANAVERAL ANYMORE

At what point does a private collection warrant its own museum?

Fred Trust took his first steps down the yellow brick road as an elementary school student in the former Soviet Union, when his teacher read a bit each day from L. Frank Baum's famous book *The Wonderful Wizard of Oz*. Trust moved to the United States, studied computer science, and raised a family before revisiting the Land of Oz while looking for something to read to his children.

He discovered that the world Baum created was vastly larger than just one book and the MGM film starring Judy Garland. There were more than a dozen novels, multiple films, and staggering quantities of memorabilia, much of which he slowly began to amass for his own private collection. It wasn't until the Smithsonian reached out to him with an interest in acquiring his collection of movie props, artwork, private journals, and other one-of-a-kind items that Trust realized he didn't want these displayed in a museum; rather he wanted a museum in which to display them—so he created one.

The Wizard of Oz Museum opened in February of 2022 and has been transporting visitors to Oz ever since. Among the items there are puppets and life-size figures, rare books, flying monkeys, dinnerware, and essentially anything else that can be

---

While you're traveling along the Space Coast seeking out strangely specific collections, add the American Police Hall of Fame & Museum in Titusville to your list.

The museum is packed with more memorabilia than you could shake a Winkie Guard spear at. Photos by Joshua Ginsberg

branded. There is also a jacket worn by Judy Garland, which she marked with her initials and, inadvertently, with the lit end of one of her cigarettes.

The pièce de résistance, however, is the immersive component. Trust applied his IT skills in developing each of several animated sequences that play on all four walls and the floor of a small theater. It allows visitors to literally walk or skip down the yellow brick road and experience for themselves iconic scenes as well as some nuances that never made it from the books to the big screen.

RUBY BEACH SANDALS

WHAT: The Wizard of Oz Museum

WHERE: 7099 N Atlantic Ave., Cape Canaveral

COST: Individual tickets are $29.99 and include the immersive experience.

PRO TIP: The immersive theater runs on a loop alternating between the Wizard of Oz and van Gogh exhibits.

DIGGING OUR HISTORY

Why were 168 bodies all buried in the exact same manner nearly 10,000 years ago?

There are some secrets in the Orlando area that date back decades. But there is one secret that dates back about 8,120 years, which is thousands of years before the Great Pyramids of Egypt were built! It's called the Windover Archeological Site and it sits west of Titusville. It was shocking enough that crews found the bodies the way they did, but even more amazing is the reason the bodies have been preserved so well.

This mystery dates back to 1982 as crews were excavating the site and a construction worker discovered a skull while digging in the boggy ground. One skull led to several more and the project was quickly halted. By the time archaeologists from Florida State University finished their work, a total of 168 bodies had been unearthed. That's when a full-blown investigation began to figure out who the people were and why they were all in such an unusual burial location. Making things more interesting is that the bodies were all buried on their left side with their heads to the west and their faces pointing north.

According to researchers, bones will typically degrade beyond recognition in about 500 years, yet these were intact after thousands of years. Not only were the bones still in good shape, but surrounding tissues also survived. It was discovered that the mucky water was a perfect place to bury the dead (at least for modern human purposes) because it slowed the deterioration process and allowed for research to be done. There isn't much

WINDOVER ARCHAEOLOGICAL SITE

WHAT: Burial site of 168 bodies more than 8,000 years ago

WHERE: The pond is one mile southeast of the I-95 and Hwy. 50 intersection.

COST: Free

PRO TIP: Only a historical marker is at the location.

The swampy area near I-95 in Brevard County where the remains of 168 people were discovered buried in the muck by a construction worker.

WINDOVER ARCHAEOLOGICAL SITE

Discovered by accident in 1982, the Windover site is a burial place of Early Native Americans who inhabited this region 7,000 to 8,000 years ago. The burials were placed underwater in the peat of the shallow pond. This peat helped to preserve normally perishable artifacts and human tissues. The site contains the largest skeletal sample in the New World and the oldest bottle gourd found north of Mexico—two features that add to its significance. It also includes the largest and most complex sample of early textiles in the New World, a pollen record from the end of the Pleistocene to Recent Eras and recovery of some of the oldest DNA from brain tissue and bone. The remarkable state of preservation has allowed archaeologists to reconstruct some of the earliest New World diets based on contents from their stomachs and on scientific analysis. The site has produced the largest and most complex textile collection ever recovered from an Early Archaic period site. It also yielded a remarkable organic artifact inventory including wood and fibers. Archaeologists from Florida State University were among those who explored the Windover site.

A FLORIDA HERITAGE SITE
SPONSORED BY THE BREVARD COUNTY HISTORICAL COMMISSION
AND THE FLORIDA DEPARTMENT OF STATE
F-486   2002

to see at the location anymore, but that land has been bought by a preservation group so it will remain undeveloped.

Windover opened the doors to the Archaic period in Florida. Similar burial sites have now been discovered in Sarasota County, Collier County, and Hardee County, all dating back thousands of years.

KEEPING WATCH ON AN ISLAND

Why is there an owl totem pole at the state park only accessible by boat?

This is one of those secrets that you really have to work at in order to see it. The owl totem pole is on Hontoon Island, which is located down a long, winding road in the middle of the St. Johns River near DeLand and can only be accessed from the water. Legend has it the early Native American settlers lived on this 1,650-acre island thousands of years ago and you can still see the remnants of their activities scattered throughout the park. But the totem pole took another twist when it was learned that the wrong tribe was likely getting credit for the carvings for decades.

Workers discovered the structure while dredging for a yacht basin in 1955 and knew they had come across something unique. The totem pole was taken to Gainesville for study at the University of Florida and it was determined that it was likely done by the Timacuan people around AD 1350, although later analysis showed it to be from the Mayacans. The owl has some human characteristics, which could

---

The St. Johns River is one of the only major waterways in the United States that flows north. And this is certainly a lazy river. From its source in Melbourne to where it enters the ocean near Jacksonville, it only drops about 30 feet, which is less than an inch per mile.

Hontoon Island State Park is right in the middle of the St. Johns River not far from DeLand. After flooding from Hurricane Ian in 2022, the park is being rebuilt and remodeled. Photo courtesy of Florida Department of Environmental Protection

HONTOON ISLAND STATE PARK

WHAT: Primitive island to explore

WHERE: 2309 River Ridge Rd., DeLand

COST: No fee to enter the park, although you will likely need to take the ferry

PRO TIP: If you decided to stay overnight, this is certainly not "glamping." The cabins have running water, electricity, ceiling fans, and bunk beds, but you will get a true taste of the Florida outdoors.

lead people to believe it was an owl changing into a human, or a human changing into an owl, but the actual meaning is lost to history. A replica of the owl totem pole was later placed back on the island.

There is plenty to do on the island once you are able to get there by private boat or ferry. This lush tropical paradise is surrounded by three different waterways: the St. Johns River, Hontoon Dead River, and Snake Creek. There is a visitors center that gives you the lay of the land for when you are ready to take a trek on the dozens of hiking trails. And if a day on the island isn't enough, you can even do some island camping in the park's primitive cabins.

A SPIRITED DISCUSSION

Why did a piece of land near Orlando become the "Psychic Capital of the World"?

A prophecy way back in the 1800s led to the founding of a camp that became the "Psychic Capital of the World" in the backwoods of central Florida. Many people driving along Interstate 4 probably have no idea that they are passing a town that is populated with certified mediums and healers about 30 miles north of Orlando. So, if you are into the supernatural and the metaphysical, you owe it to yourself to check out the town of Cassadaga.

People come from all over the world to experience the Cassadaga Spiritualist Camp to get a better understanding of spirituality, but few people actually live there. When you walk the streets in the metaphysical district, you can truly feel something is different about this 35-acre plot of land. Maybe it's the calmness that brings everyone down—or up—a level. There are only 55 residences in the historic district with approximately 35 mediums residing in that small area. And if you want to rub elbows with people who talk with spirits and see the world in a different light, the church services at Cassadaga Spiritualist Camp need to be on your list.

There are also a few parks and walking trails around the town including Horseshoe Park and Fairy Trail. The trail takes you into the woods where you come upon all sorts of surprises. Miniature

CASSADAGA SPIRITUALIST CAMP

WHAT: Psychic Capital of the World

WHERE: Cassadaga

COST: It is free to roam the historic district and stores. Psychic readings can be purchased throughout the town.

PRO TIP: Stop as soon as you see the Cassadaga Spiritualist Camp Bookstore and the Cassadaga Hotel to start your excursion. Most of the interesting places are within walking distance of these two buildings.

Psychics and mediums have businesses all over the Cassadaga Spiritualist Camp.
It is known as the "Psychic Capital of the World." Photo by Lauren Brown

homes and small establishments appear to be the residences of pixies, gnomes, and sprites. And if that is not your thing, the walk through the woods certainly brings a sense of calm.

There is no cemetery in Cassadaga, although there is one nearby in Lake Helen. In that cemetery is a legend of a Devil's Chair, which is a brick bench near the grave of a child. Legend has it that there is often paranormal activity there and if you leave an unopened can of beer on the bench it will be empty come morning. Others say that if you sit in the chair, you can sometimes hear the devil talking directly to you.

WHERE THE SURF GLOWS UNDER THE FULL MOON

Does the ocean really glow at certain times of the year near the Space Coast?

A trip along the Indian River Lagoon near the Kennedy Space Center is always "out of this world." But in the summer months, it truly is magical. It's called bioluminescence and it's something that happens in only a few places on earth. And yes, the water does actually glow. But contrary to popular belief, you don't have to have a bright moon to see it. Many times, it glows even brighter when there is less light overhead.

Bioluminescence is basically when water organisms like dinoflagellates (or plankton) give off light under the water, much like fireflies do. You may even see some glowing jellyfish! When your paddle or hand comes in contact with the bioluminescent organisms, it causes them to glow in a blue-green hue. June through October is when it is most likely to happen in the intracoastal waters of Brevard County like the Indian River Lagoon, Banana River, and Mosquito Lagoon.

A daytime excursion on the Canaveral National Seashore is a treat anytime, day or night. The national park encompasses more than 50,000 acres of lagoons, islands, and offshore waters. You will see everything from endangered turtles, alligators, manatees, dolphins, and some of the most amazing waterfowl you can find on the planet, all in one place.

Glass-bottom kayaks are some of the best ways to experience the waters along the coast of Florida. It's extra special when bioluminescence is taking place. Photo by Teresa Brown

GLASS-BOTTOM KAYAK TOUR

WHAT: An excursion to see the waters light up at night

WHERE: Point of entry varies along the Canaveral National Seashore.

COST: Approximately $75 depending on tour

PRO TIP: Book early because these trips fill up quickly.

You can often see it from the shore, but your best bet is to get out onto the water and see it up close and personal. There are several kayak and paddleboard excursions you can book a trip with and it's best to find a time closest to the new moon when it's the most spectacular. You are also likely to see manatees and dolphins rising to the surface under the stars in the middle of the water, which makes the trip even more memorable.

ONE FOR THE ROAD

What Port Orange bar calls itself the "home of ice-cold beer and killer women"?

Fueled by psychosis, anathema to civilized society, and featured prominently in best-selling books and box-office blockbusters, serial killers are a fact of modern life. While each of their sordid stories is unique, data suggests some commonalities, including gender: nearly 90 percent of known serial murderers over the last century have been male. But Aileen Wuornos was one of the rare exceptions. From 1989 to 1990, she made central Florida her hunting ground, and she made the Last Resort biker bar in Port Orange an occasional watering hole, where she kept a low profile. It was there on the evening of January 19, 1991, that Wuornos was arrested on an outstanding warrant. From there she was convicted of murder, sentenced to death, and executed in 2002. Though she never again saw the inside of the Last Resort, in some ways, she has also never left the establishment.

Inside the bar, you can find various framed pictures of Wuornos, and if owner Al Bulling is there he might share some stories. On one of the walls there's a painting of Wuornos by artist Ted E. Bear alongside a list of her seven victims. The bar has even created its own "Crazy Killer Hot Sauce," which some may find in poor taste (while others shrug and say it tastes just fine).

Some claim that she lives on in the bar in more than just memories and marketing gimmicks—shortly after her execution, patrons and staff began having a variety of paranormal experiences including strange orbs of light, objects moving of

COLD AS ICE

WHAT: The Last Resort Bar

WHERE: 5812 S Ridgewood Ave., Port Orange

COST: You can have lunch and a couple beers for all of about $20—less than some of the Wuornos merchandise.

PRO TIP: Things get very loud and busy there during Bike Week. Plan accordingly.

The Last Resort Bar is often more of a first choice among bikers and those interested in serial killer Aileen Wuornos. Photos by Joshua Ginsberg

their own accord, and a bell that still rings on its own from time to time.

Was she a victim, a monster, or maybe both? Is she now a ghost haunting the Last Resort? We'll leave you to decide.

For her portrayal of Wuornos as a deeply disturbed and complex character in the 2003 film *Monster*, Charlize Theron earned an Academy Award for Best Actress in a Leading Role.

THE RUINS OF NSB

What are the two sets of ruins located in New Smyrna Beach?

The areas comprising what is now known as New Smyrna Beach have a fascinating history. The settlement dates back to 1768 and the town was incorporated in 1887. The founder was a physician named Andrew Turnbull, who named the city using the word Smyrna, which was an homage to his wife's heritage in Greece. Much of the city's history is well established, but there are often questions about the two sets of ruins located in the city.

HISTORIC RUINS

WHAT: New Smyrna Sugar Mill Ruins

WHERE: 600 Mission Dr., New Smyrna Beach

COST: Free

PRO TIP: Visit the New Smyrna Museum of History prior to the ruins to learn more about the history of the area. It will make the trips much more meaningful and insightful.

These sugar mill ruins are about a mile west of the intracoastal waterway and date back to 1830. It was a dual-purpose facility that functioned as a steam-operated sugar mill and sawmill. But it only lasted five years and was destroyed by Native Americans during the Second Seminole War. Some of the walls remain erect and the site has been added to the US National Register of Historic Places.

The second set of ruins are truly a mystery. The unfinished coquina labyrinth known as the Turnbull Ruins still stand not far from the Canal Historic District and the intracoastal waterway. The structure is made of coquina, which is a concrete-like structure made of rock and shell fragments. It was named after Dr. Turnbull, and some believe it was the foundation of his mansion or possibly a church. Others believe it predates Turnbull's arrival. Whatever it was, it's worth a few minutes of time to explore for yourself.

The ruins of the Old Sugar Mill still stand in New Smyrna Beach. Even though much is gone, it's still easy to follow the historical process of how they operated. Photos by John Brown

And if you want to throw in one more mystery, what's up with that grave right in the middle of Canova Drive? That is actually the burial site of Charles Dummett who was a child who died while hunting back in 1861 and was buried at the spot. When developers began building on that part of New Smyrna Beach, they simply routed the road around his grave.

New Smyrna Beach is billed by *National Geographic* as "one of the top 20 surf towns" and is also known as the "shark bite capital of the world." Surf very carefully!

THE PATH OF ENLIGHTENMENT

Where can you find inner peace along with the four largest statues of Buddha in Florida?

Visitors come to the Space Coast from around the world for a glimpse into the vast expanse beyond our planet. Most of these individuals are entirely unaware that just miles from the Cape Canaveral launchpads, at the end of a winding gravel road, is a different sort of place, dedicated to transcending boundaries via the exploration of inner rather than outer space.

Since its formation in 2005, the 30-acre Vietnamese Buddhist monastery known as the White Sands Buddhist Center has been open to the public from dawn to dusk, welcoming the curious as well as the devout. In 2006 a series of structures was erected, including a temple, a house for the monks and nuns, a dining hall, a meditation area, and a gift shop. The center's real claim to fame arrived in 2012, in the form of three massive granite statues of different Buddhas. The 60-ton reclining Nirvana Buddha (depicting Siddhartha at age 80, just prior to his death) stretches 35 feet long, the 62-ton Mother of Avalokitesvara (bodhisattva of peace and compassion) stands 32 feet tall, and the meditating Shakyamuni Buddha measures 35 feet tall and weighs in at over 200 tons. A fourth, 35-foot-tall statue of a baby Buddha was added more recently in 2017.

If Mims is a bit too far to travel, you could visit the Guang Ming Temple or the Chua Bao An Buddhist Temple, both of which are in Orlando.

Visitors reflect on both a Buddha statue and the surface of the pond. Photo by Joshua Ginsberg

LIVING IN HARMONY

WHAT: White Sands Buddhist Center

WHERE: 4640 Knost Dr., Mims

COST: Free to visit

PRO TIP: Every step of the journey is the journey. This particular journey, however, is intended only for human beings so please leave your pets at home.

Following the path from one statue to the next leads past smaller statues, a bodhi tree, a reflecting pool, a brass prayer bell, benches, and a variety of messages in both English and Vietnamese for thoughtful, self-directed contemplation. More structured meditation services are held on Sunday mornings from 10 a.m. to noon, and for those seeking a more active approach to Buddhist teachings, Wednesdays at 11 a.m. volunteers are invited to participate in weekly grounds-keeping activities. Guided tours are also available and can be arranged prior to visiting.

RACING FROM THE BEGINNING

Is there really a hotel where NASCAR was born?

Most people are well aware of the massive Daytona International Speedway and how much it means to the Daytona Beach area. And most are also likely aware that the early Daytona 500 races actually took place on the actual beach. But few people know that there is a hotel near the beach where drivers and officials first met to discuss the idea of devising a racing league that became NASCAR.

The Streamline Hotel opened in 1941 on South Atlantic Avenue not far from what became known as the "World's Most Famous Beach." Of course, that hotel played a large part in the beach becoming so well known. A mere seven years after the hotel opened for business, an official NASCAR-sanctioned race took place just blocks away from where the organization was born. The hotel became such a big hit that well-known guests like Al Capone stayed there during its initial heyday.

The hotel fell on hard times and went from an icon to an eyesore. Developer Eddie Hennessy bought the hotel in 2014, refurbished it into a beautiful getaway, and truly took NASCAR roots to heart.

STREAMLINE HOTEL

WHAT: Historic hotel where NASCAR was born

WHERE: 140 S Atlantic Ave., Daytona Beach

COST: Rooms start at $125 per night.

PRO TIP: Not far from the hotel is the historic Racing's North Turn restaurant. That is where the racers turned around during the races. It's worth the trip to complete your NASCAR-inspired vacation.

Everything inside the hotel is now an homage to NASCAR and has become a tourist attraction for not only race fans but for drivers too. From iconic pictures of the early meetings of executives to authentic race memorabilia, the Streamline Hotel's secret past is now coming of age.

Daytona Beach was named after one of the early landowners, Matthias Day. He owned more than 3,000 acres of land, which he bought in 1870 for $1,200. The three towns of Daytona, Daytona Beach, and Seabreeze later merged together to form the much larger Daytona Beach in 1926.

The Streamline Hotel in Daytona Beach is where NASCAR was born. This is the spot where early leaders of the sport met to come up with a racing league. Photo by Sophia Brown

ALL THAT AND A BAG OF CHIPS

What might it look like if a video/bookstore-café-bar-restaurant was decorated by the Cure's Robert Smith?

The last decade of the 20th century (aka the '90s) was a great many strange things to those who experienced it—Mulder and Scully were introducing home audiences to paranormal investigation, streaming had yet to put the "bust" in Blockbuster, the federal government was trying to figure out how Microsoft bundled its software, and the rest of the country was learning how to pronounce Lollapalooza. There was also a new thing called the internet, but using it required connecting through a modem and listening to the sounds of a robot being tortured to death.

Appropriately, Stardust Video & Coffee (a shout-out to Woody Allen's *Stardust Memories*), opened in 1999 by Brett and Katherine Bennett, has also been a great many things, starting with a shop serving coffee and baked goods and renting videos. Two years later they opened a full kitchen with beer; wine; and a literature-, film-, and music-inspired menu (featuring items including the Rob Reiner, American Psycho, and Crispin Glover). In 2010 they started serving liquor (from both the Slanted & Enchanted Bar in the large room and the smaller Scotch bar). Along the way they added books and local art for sale, a photo booth, and a stage for live music and events.

While there's a strong, eclectic retro vibe (is that a Snoopy Sno-Cone Machine on the wall?), it might not be entirely

JUST LIKE HEAVEN

WHAT: Stardust Video & Coffee

WHERE: 1842 Winter Park Rd.

COST: Generally very reasonably priced, but some of those Scotches can get expensive.

PRO TIP: The "Stoner" (coffee with butter, brown sugar, and honey) is a perennial favorite.

The stage and bar inside Stardust Video & Coffee. Photos by Joshua Ginsberg

accurate to say that its "theme" is specific only to the '90s. A far better description, often repeated by staff and patrons, is that Stardust is Orlando's very own "Island of Misfit Toys" where all manner of oddities (human and otherwise) are welcome. Like Doug Rhodehamel and the photo behind the bar of his Cream Cheese Jesus Miracle Knife—be sure to inquire about that one.

Wally's Bar and Liquors is another much-loved local watering hole with plenty of character. You can still find former owner Wally Updike there, but he isn't much for conversation these days—his ashes are kept in a corner alcove.

FIBERGLASS MENAGERIE

What's with all the strange roadside statues in Gotha?

With a population just shy of 2,000 (as of the 2010 census), Gotha, Florida, doesn't see as much foot traffic from visitors as other nearby towns and cities. But what it lacks in population, it makes up for in quirkiness, specifically along Eighth Avenue in a residential neighborhood.

Here a collection of unexpected and incongruous statues line the roadside. The "Gotha Statue Parade," as it's known locally, begins with a detachment of Roman soldiers and a horse-drawn chariot. Next in line is a collection of animals native to Africa including elephants, lions, giraffes, zebras, and a ram for good measure. Farther along the street is an assortment of angels alongside a crucified Jesus (a noncrucified version can be found toward the very end of the street past the snowman), children playing with a family of bears, and other unusual displays.

The newer statues, like the Roman soldiers, very likely made the march to their present site from the now defunct Holy Land

Experience. Other statues appear to have been there much longer and have seen better days—some have toppled over, broken in places, or could just use a good cleaning and a fresh coat of paint.

Why are they there? What does it mean? Is it the remnants of an amusement park that never came to

North of Orlando in Pierson is another strange roadside display and curio shop known as the Barberville Yard Art Emporium. It's hard to miss—just look for the 20-foot-tall giraffe towering over the dinosaurs and aliens.

An odd and unexplained roadside safari in Gotha. Photos by Joshua Ginsberg

BLOCK PARTY

WHAT: The Gotha Statue Parade

WHERE: 9925–9957 8th St., Gotha

COST: Free

PRO TIP: If you work up an appetite there, stop off at Yellow Dog Eats, located in downtown Gotha's historic Brockman House. As the name implies, you can bring Fido.

fruition, the start of a religious-themed outsider art park, or maybe just an alternative to pink flamingos for lawn decorations? Rather than ponder its deeper significance (assuming there is any), why not take the short drive from Orlando and puzzle over it in person? Even if you don't come to any profound conclusions, you'll certainly get some interesting vacation photos that don't involve any Disney characters.

If you visit, remember to be respectful—the statues stand on private property.

161

MONKEY BUSINESS AT THE SPRINGS

Are the purest waters in the world found near Ocala, and why are there monkeys there?

The Silver Springs in Marion County aren't perfect, but they are about as close as you can get. You have probably seen the images on social media of the turquoise waters where you can see the sandy bottom in picture-perfect clarity. And according to studies, they are 99.8 percent pure. So, if there is something better, it can't be by much.

Silver Springs is actually the conglomeration of seven major springs that pump out about 550 million gallons of 72-degree water every day. As amazing as that may sound, the "age" of the water may be even more astonishing. Rain that falls today will have to work its way through the sand, soil, then limestone and deep into the Florida aquifer before it becomes a part of the spring system and pushed back to earth. That

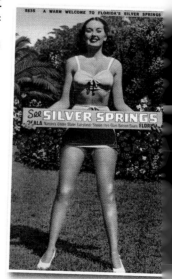

water we are seeing today has been underground for two decades!

Admiring the water from the shore is one thing, but the best way to see "Florida's Oldest Attraction" is on board the world-famous glass-bottomed boats. This attraction near Ocala has been drawing crowds since the 1800s and is

SILVER SPRINGS STATE PARK

WHAT: Excursion through a beautiful Florida park

WHERE: 5656 E Silver Springs Blvd., Silver Springs

COST: $8 per vehicle to enter the park. Glass Bottom Boat tours range from $12 to $25.

PRO TIP: Watch old videos of the *Sea Hunt* TV show to build the anticipation. Many parts of the series were shot on location at Silver Springs.

Silver Springs State Park has been a Florida attraction for decades. Numerous shows and movies have been shot on the property. But one of the biggest thrills is seeing the monkeys living in the trees.

even the beautiful backdrop to movies like *Creature from the Black Lagoon* and *Tarzan*.

The park is also home to about 400 rhesus macaques, which are descendants from monkeys that were released back in the 1930s to increase tourism for the jungle boat cruises. A local legend claims they escaped during the taping of *Tarzan Finds a Son* in 1939, but that appears to be just a tale. So a canoe trip along the river is an adventure that you likely won't experience anywhere else.

There are 175 Florida state parks. The state has won the honor of the best state park system in the country four times.

HIDDEN IN
THE HAMMOCK

**Where can you see Florida as it was before
the tourists arrived?**

Old Florida at its finest! Many people who visit—or even live
in—Orlando often want to see what the area looked like before
the 1970s when it turned into a tourist mecca. As more people
move to central Florida, there are fewer places that have kept
the "old Florida" look and feel. But you really don't have to travel
very far to still feel like you are getting in touch with that part of
history and nature. The Black Hammock Wilderness Area and
nearby Black Hammock Adventures are about as "old Florida"
as you would want to get and still have running water and air-
conditioning.

This Black Hammock Wilderness Area is a 700-acre nature
preserve tucked away near Oviedo down a few small roads and
way back in the trees along the banks of Lake Jesup. That's
where you can go for a hike to see areas that are untouched for
thousands of years. But if you want to fully take in natural Florida,
you have to hit the water at the nearby entertainment complex
with a similar name, Black Hammock Adventures.

And yes, we are talking about "the" Lake Jesup, which is
billed as the "most gator-infested lake in the world." Lake Jesup

---

Nearby Oviedo is known for its wild chickens
roaming the downtown area. The locals are
crazy about the birds, too. There are about
a dozen or so chickens roaming around and
they get the rock-star treatment. In fact, when
a recent chicken was killed by a wild animal,
the town had a memorial service for him.

Airboat tours, like this one at the Black Hammock, show how Florida used to look and how it's changing today. Photo by Mike Brown

THE BLACK HAMMOCK NATURE PRESERVE

WHAT: Nature excursion to see "old Florida"

WHERE: 2316 Black Hammock Fish Camp Rd., Oviedo

COST: The nature preserve is free. Airboat rides are $35 for adults and $30 for kids.

PRO TIP: You will want to do it all at Black Hammock. Plan on getting there in the afternoon for a boat ride, check out the collection of exotic animals, then stick around for dinner and drinks.

is where wildlife officials dump so-called "nuisance gators." At last estimate, there are over 9,500 alligators in the 10,000-acre lake, so the odds of seeing one (or many) are very good. You may also see bald eagles, exotic birds, wild boars, and even bobcats on the shore as you travel through the ancient hammock with trees that are thousands of years old.

SWIRLED DOMINATION

What Disney partnership produced a snack with its own cult following?

Gatorade was invented in Gainesville. The Camel Rider sandwich is unique to Jacksonville. Both Tampa and Miami lay claim to the Cuban sandwich. There's Swamp Cabbage, Key lime pie, Sour Orange Pie, Gator Bites, conch fritters (a true testament to mankind's ability to deep fry anything), and a smorgasbord of other foods that could only have originated in Florida.

None of these though have anything remotely close to the massive and obsessive following that Dole Whip has accrued.

The story began in 1963 when Walt Disney's Enchanted Tiki Room made its debut in Disneyland, which was joined five years later by the Tiki Juice Bar. In 1976, when DOLE became a corporate sponsor of both the Tiki Room and the Juice Bar, the latter began serving pineapple spears and juice, which evolved into soft-serve ice cream topped with pineapples. In 1983, DOLE also became a sponsor of Walt Disney World Resort, at which point it tasked food scientist Kathy Westphal with devising a version of their frozen treat that could handle the Florida heat.

In 1984, the first official Dole Whip was served at Disney World's Magic Kingdom Park (and subsequently at Disneyland),

The authentic and original "Dole Whip" as served at the Polynesian Village Resort. Photo by Joshua Ginsberg

and its popularity vastly exceeded expectations. Now more than 40 years after its introduction, Disney Parks and Resorts sell over 3.4 million cups annually. When lemon became the seventh flavor of Dole Whip, people waited in lines for up to an hour to get a taste.

Up until just recently, the authentic "Dole Whip" was only offered through Disney. In March of 2023, Dole announced that as part of a larger company rebranding, it would be making three flavors of Dole Whip available at grocery stores and venues. While many fans of the frozen treat will be happy to hear this, some, no doubt, will reject such a move, insisting that no matter what it calls itself, Dole Whip served anywhere but a Disney property is really just pineapple soft-serve.

ON THE DOLE

WHAT: Dole Whip (the "official" version)

WHERE: Aloha Isle and Sunshine Tree Terrace in the Magic Kingdom, Pineapple Lanai and Oasis Bar and Grill inside Disney's Polynesian Village Resort, Snack Shack at Disney's Typhoon Lagoon, Tamu Tamu Refreshments in Disney's Animal Kingdom, and both Swirls on the Water and Wine Bar George at Disney Springs

COST: $6.49 for a Dole Whip dessert and $7.29 for a Dole Whip Float, as of this writing

PRO TIP: If Disney-specific foods are your thing, you can also try the Mickey-shaped pretzels, waffles, beignets and ice cream bars, and a cookie from Gideon's Bakehouse

In 1997, Disney and McDonald's entered into a relationship that made McFlurries, chicken McNuggets, and fries available in all four parks. The contract was not renewed, and all but one location serving McDonald's in the parks were phased out.

A GHOST OF A CHANCE

What are the mysterious lights seen floating near the Econlockhatchee River?

If you were ever looking for a good ghost story, it might be worth the drive down Snow Hill Road in the nature area between Oviedo, Chuluota, and Geneva. Many people will say the Oviedo Ghost Lights, or the Chuluota Lights, are just a myth, but others swear they have seen them. These sightings have been going on for decades, so likely there is something in the air. But what, exactly, is still a mystery.

Some locals say the balls of light hover over the road on various nights throughout the year as you approach and then cross the bridge over the Econlockhatchee River. Police have even been notified by drivers over the years that the lights chased their cars for a short time and then simply disappeared. They became so prevalent in the 1960s and '70s that researchers even went out to try and determine what they were. Scientists say they are likely caused by some sort of reaction with swamp gases and light reflections causing the illusion, but nothing official has ever been determined.

Because the lights are so hit and miss, people also head to Oviedo to check out the chickens roaming around the city. The fowl first started appearing downtown in the early 1800s. Since then, the population has grown and the brood has become a part of the landscape. Heck, they even have their own Facebook page. You can often see "city-folk" stopping by to take pictures

GHOSTLY GASES

WHAT: Oviedo Ghost Lights

WHERE: Highway 419 at the Econ River Bridge east of Oviedo

COST: Free

PRO TIP: Most sightings of the Ghost Lights happen during warmer months. This may make sense if the lights are in fact glowing swamp gases being released by the earth around the river.

The bridge over the Little Econ River near Oviedo. Mysterious lights have been reported floating above the roadway, especially in warmer months. Photo by Lauren Brown

and feed the birds. And if the kids have never actually been to a barnyard, they might be shocked to get this close to the farm. The entire city is actually classified as a bird sanctuary because of the feathered friends.

The Econlockhatchee River is a short river with a long name. Locals simply call it the Econ River to keep it simple. Even the name is a mystery, but basically means "Rivers of Mounds" due to the abundance of Native American mounds near the stream.

SPOOK HILL IN LAKE WALES

Why do cars appear to be rolling uphill on Spook Hill?

This mysterious spot on a road in Lake Wales has become world famous and spawned countless arguments as well as explanations. It's known as "Spook Hill" and it even has a legend that includes a giant alligator and a Native American warrior that were killed in a massive battle that caused the swampy depression that generates all the interest. That story is one part of the legend, but the next part revolves around early settlers whose horses had troubles walking through the area. Then there is the legend of Florida pirate Captain Sasparilla, buried on the hill, who is pushing the cars away. Of course, with no other explanation, it eventually became known as Spook Hill.

SPOOK HILL

WHAT: Optical illusion where cars appear to be rolling uphill

WHERE: 600 N Wales Dr., Lake Wales

COST: Free

PRO TIP: If you are leaving from Orlando, this is a pretty good drive and won't take long to explore. You may want to find another attraction along the way to make a day trip, like the Bok Tower Gardens.

The nearby Bok Tower Gardens is a National Historic Landmark. It's named after Edward Bok, the editor of *Ladies' Home Journal*, who lived there after his retirement. It's one of the highest points in Florida, and the sounds of the carillon ringing through the trees is as close to heaven as you can find on earth.

Spook Hill has been an iconic attraction for decades. Yes, you have to use a little imagination, but you will see cars testing the spirits throughout the day. Photo by John Brown

Now fast-forward to the age of the automobile and factor in gravity and an optical illusion, and you see the next part of this legend. What makes the hill "spooky" today is that when you put your car in neutral on the stretch of road signified with the giant sign and white stripe on the pavement, it begins to roll "uphill" as if something, or someone, is pulling the vehicle toward the hill's crest. There is actually a scientific explanation of that part of the legend, which is part optical illusion and part "gravity hill," but that would ruin the fun of experiencing it yourself.

This area became legendary in the post–World War II era as families began to travel in the automobile age and it took on a life of its own. The National Park Service has designated the location as a significant entertainment destination, and the nearby school is even named Spook Hill Elementary.

Who knows, maybe the gator, warrior, pirate, early pioneers, and today's drivers are all caught up in the same central Florida secret! As the sign with the friendly ghost near the site reads, "Is it the gator seeking revenge, or the chief protecting his land?"

THE MONSTERS AT THE END OF THIS BOOK

In a world gone geek, how does one pop-culture store keep taking its game to the next level?

There are lots of comic books stores and retailers offering sci-fi, fantasy, role-playing, and anime-related collectibles and merchandise, but there is only one Gods & Monsters. So what makes this self-described "Nerd Hub" truly epic (as proven by scores of Best in Orlando awards)? Here's a short list:

1. Cover all the bases: Whatever convention or fandom brings you to town, you will find it well represented here. From *Star Wars* and *Star Trek* to Marvel, DC, and independent comics, to *Supernatural*, anime and manga, *X-Files*, *Ghostbusters*, *Game of Thrones*, *Dr. Who*, video games (spanning Atari to MMORGs), Magic the Gathering, Transformers, Farscape, Shadowrun, and so on, ad infinitum.

2. Call in an old friend: Wondering about that massive selection of rare and autographed Neil Gaiman goods? Turns out he has a long and close relationship with the owners and helped in opening the store. Having a big name involved never hurts.

The Dragon Vault, an immersive fantasy-themed restaurant and bar featuring meat served on swords and potion cocktails, is expected to open the doors to its lair in the 100-year-old Wells Fargo Building in Sanford sometime in late 2023. Check online for updates and details.

All the comics, RPG game gear, and geeky toys you wish you'd had as a kid. Or as an adult. No judgment here. Photos by Joshua Ginsberg

ROLE FOR INITIATIVE

WHAT: Gods & Monsters

WHERE: 5421 International Dr.

COST: Free to browse, but the life-size models fetch a Mandalorian-sized bounty.

PRO TIP: Let the Wookie win.

3. Add a gamer bar: If you like to "drink and know things" in true Lannister fashion, take a seat inside Vault 5421 (that's a *Fallout* reference). There you can enjoy a drink themed around the latest installment of *Stranger Things*, *The Lord of the Rings*, or whatever's happening at the moment. You can also join a party for Dungeons & Dragons & Drinks with ready-made character sheets, or party it up with cosplayers.

4. Inclusivity for the win: One of the store's most popular offerings is its wide selection of LGBTQ+ and minority-created comics and graphic novels. Visitors will also find local artwork displayed throughout the store.

Can't find what you're looking for? Just ask. The folks there might not be able to tell James T. Kirk exactly what God needs with a starship, but odds are good that they could help him procure one.

Rock Springs Run, Kelly Park

SOURCES

Orlando's Legendary Literary Launchpad: https://www.kerouacproject.org/history/.

The Hidden Highway to Florida: https://floridatraveler.com/florida-ghost-highway/; https://howwefindhappy.com/florida-historic-old-dixie-highway/travel/; https://en.wikipedia.org/wiki/Dixie_Highway.

Ancient Reptile Visit: None

If You Build It, They Will Come: https://www.orlando.gov/Our-Government/History/Find-Historic-Landmarks/Tinker-Field/Tinker-Field; https://www.orlando.gov/Our-Government/Departments-Offices/Executive-Offices/Office-of-Multicultural-Affairs/The-Fabric-of-Our-Communities-Black-Historical-Sites/Tinker-Field-History-Plaza/Tinker-Field-History-Plaza.

Of Crocs and Crackers: https://www.roadsideamerica.com/story/68688#:~:text=According%20to%20local%20lore%2C%20a,time%20was%20a%20dirt%20street; https://www.orlandosentinel.com/news/os-xpm-2003-08-10-0308090119-story.html.

Tombs of the Well-Known: https://www.orlandosentinel.com/news/os-xpm-2012-10-30os-greenwood-cemetery-tour-orlando-20121016-story.html; https://www.orlando.gov/Our-Government/Departments-Offices/Executive-Offices/City-Clerk/Greenwood-Cemetery.

A City by Any Other Name: https://myfloridahistory.org/frontiers/article/13; https://www.orlandosentinel.com/news/os-xpm-1998-01-18-9801161380-story.html; https://www.orlando.gov/Our-Government/History.

Murder Most Fowl: https://www.thehistorycenter.org/billy/; https://www.yourcommunitypaper.com/articles/the-way-we-were-billy-bluebeard-the-tyrant-swan-of-lake-lucerne/.

An Escape under Orange Avenue: https://en.wikipedia.org/wiki/Beacham_Theatre#cite_note-Guida2014-67; https://www.orlandomagazine.com/answer-man-22/.

Swimming in Secrets: https://luckyslakeswim.com/.

The City Hauntingly Beautiful: None

Built to Last: https://www.wellsbuilt.org/; https://med.ucf.edu/news/black-history-month-talk-highlights-one-of-orlandos-first-black-doctors/; https://www.clickorlando.com/features/2020/02/28/a-building-unchanged-wells-built-museum-highlights-orlandos-black-history-year-round/.

Rockin' in the Free World: https://orlandotouristinformationbureau.com/touristinfo/Hard-Rock-Cafe-Orlando-Secret-Tour.htm; https://insidethemagic.net/2021/12/berlin-wall-resides-universal-orlando-ab1/; https://www.mynews13.com/fl/orlando/news/2019/11/08/where-to-see-a-piece-of-the-berlin-wall-in-orlando.

The Unbelievably True Storage: None

Old Records Never Die: None

Rising from the Ashes: https://www.orlandomagazine.com/mathers-social-gathering-parlor-chic/; https://www.hiddenlibations.com/mathers-social-gathering-floridas-largest-speakeasy/.

A Night to Remember: https://titanicorlando.com/visit/.

Dust Tracks on the Road to Eatonville: https://www.soulofamerica.com/us-cities/orlando/eatonvile-zora-neale-hurston/; https://www.visitflorida.com/listing/the-zora-neale-hurston-national-museum-of-fine-arts/23950/; https://cityoffortpierce.com/412/Timeline-of-Zora-Neale-Hurston.

Pineapple Express: https://orlandoretro.com/2013/11/01/pineapples-water-parks-and-the-history-of-lake-ivanhoe/; https://guide.michelin.com/us/en/florida/orlando/restaurant/the-pinery; https://orlandomemory.info/places/college-park-historic-homes-tour-shore-crest-1996/.

Escaping the Doldrums: https://disney.fandom.com/wiki/Trader_Sam%27s; https://societyofexplorersandadventurers.fandom.com/wiki/Trader_Sam%27s_Grog_Grotto; https://www.disneyfoodblog.com/2021/07/19/shhhh-there-are-3-secret-drinks-at-trader-sams-in-disney-world/.

African Safari near Main Street USA: https://disneyworld.disney.go.com/events-tours/animal-kingdom/wild-africa-trek/; https://www.wdwinfo.com/walt-disney-world/animal-kingdom/the-wildest-experience-at-walt-disney-world-wild-africa-trek/.

Murals with a Mission: https://www.clickorlando.com/weather/2018/08/09/monarch-initiative-paints-curiosity-about-declining-butterfly-population/; https://inkdwell.com/monarch-butterfly/.

"Train"ing the Guests: https://cityofwinterpark.org/government/about/history/; https://parkplazahotel.com/.

Messages Hiding in Plain Sight: https://nonahoodnews.com/the-artist-jefre/#:~:text=Jefr%C3%AB%20moved%20to%20Lake%20Nona,competitions%20all%20over%20the%20world; https://www.lakenona.com/story-article/lake-nona-art-tour/.

An All-Inclusive Stay: https://www.msn.com/en-us/travel/article/wondering-how-to-talk-to-your-kids-about-racism-check-into-this-florida-hotel/ar-AAYBC7r?li=BBnbklE; https://www.essence.com/news/money-career/diversity-equity-inclusion-focused-hotel-opens-in-orlando/; https://www.fodors.com/world/north-america/usa/florida/orlando/experiences/news/the-childrens-library-at-lake-nona-wave-hotel-is-teaching-kids-how-to-be-anti-racist-through-books.

A Beautiful Day in the Neighborhood: https://www.rollins.edu/news/crafting-an-icon; https://en.wikipedia.org/wiki/Fred_Rogers; https://www.npr.org/2021/10/29/1050424204/mister-rogers-fred-statue-rollins-college; https://lib.rollins.edu/olin/Archives/Architecture/Arch/Walk_of_Fame.htm.

Voyages to See the VIPs: https://piershare.com/blog/floridas-inland-waterways-the-10-largest-lakes-in-the-sunshine-state; https://www.scenicboattours.com/.

No Mama, No Papa, No Uncle Sam: https://robertreddhistorian.com/bataan-corregidor-world-war-ii-monument-in-kissimmee-florida/; https://www.wftv.com/news/man-wants-ashes-buried-in-kissimmee-statue/286617341/; https://www.orlandosentinel.com/news/os-xpm-1992-05-24-9205220797-story.html.

Monumentally Unusual: https://www.atlasobscura.com/places/monument-of-states; https://www.roadsideamerica.com/story/6158; https://en.wikipedia.org/wiki/Monument_of_States.

When You Wish upon a Star: https://www.gktw.org/about/.

A Sweet Deal on Swampland: https://www.abandonedfl.com/disston-sugar-mill/.

OIA versus MCO: https://www.orlandosentinel.com/news/transportation/orl-mccoy0707oct07-story.html; https://en.wikipedia.org/wiki/Orlando_International_Airport.

Terminally Creative: https://orlandoairports.net/getting-around-mco/; https://www.orlandovillas.com/florida_guide/art-at-orlando-international-airport.aspx; https://www.seegreatart.art/florida-highwaymen-paintings-at-orlando-international-airport-terminal-c/.

Carving Out a Place for Oneself: https://polasek.org/about/albinpolasek/.

Gemütlichkeit **in Sanford:** www.willowtreecafe.com; https://growingbolder.com/stories/willow-tree-cafe/.

Haul of Fame: None

Transcendence in Opalescence: https://morsemuseum.org/plan-your-visit/chapel/; The Tiffany Chapel at the Morse Museum, A Guide, 2002, Charles Hosmer Morse Foundation, Inc.

A Horse Is a Horse, of Course, of Course: https://www.horseandriderliving.com/articles/big-bob-a-hearse-horse; http://www.weirdus.com/states/florida/cemetery_safari/horse_grave/index.php; https://florida.pbslearningmedia.org/resource/sanford-old-bob-the-horse-central-florida-roadtrip/sanford-old-bob-the-horse-central-florida-roadtrip/.

The Forgotten Florida Canal: https://www.floridastateparks.org/learn/history-cross-florida-greenway; https://en.wikipedia.org/wiki/Marjorie_Harris_Carr_Cross_Florida_Greenway; https://www.nrc.gov/docs/ML1204/ML12044A397.pdf.

Forever under the Happy Little Clouds: https://www.biography.com/news/bob-ross-biography-facts; https://en.wikipedia.org/wiki/Bob_Ross; https://www.theclio.com/entry/94433; https://allthatsinteresting.com/bob-ross-death.

Presidents Hall of Fame: https://www.roadsideamerica.com/story/20286; https://www.dailycommercial.com/story/news/local/clermont/2021/01/20/presidents-hall-of-fame-owner-john-zweifel-dies-clermont-joe-biden-white-house-wax-museum/6653284002/.

Off-Roading in the Florida Outback: https://showcaseofcitrus.com/; https://www.tripstodiscover.com/floridas-monster-truck-safari-at-showcase-of-citrus/; https://www.lakeridgewinery.com/.

The I-4 Eyesore: https://www.abandonedfl.com/majesty-building/; https://wacxtv.com/SuperChannelCentre/MajestyBuildingInformation.aspx.

Of Pachyderms and Parks: https://www.floridastateparks.org/parks-and-trails/de-leon-springs-state-park; https://beacononlinenews.com/2021/01/27/deleon-springs-performer-recalls-water-skiing-elephant-show/.

Mount Dora Catacombs: https://www.orlandosentinel.com/news/os-xpm-1991-12-22-9112220529-story.html; https://www.mountdorabuzz.com/who-knew/mount-doras-biggest-secret-the-catacombs.

These Colors Won't Run: https://authenticflorida.com/home-is-where-the-art-is-at-the-starry-night-house-in-mt-dora/.

Power, Corruption, and Lies: https://www.thehistorycenter.org/mabel-norris-reese/; https://www.dailycommercial.com/story/news/local/mount-dora/2021/09/24/bust-journalist-mabel-norris-reese-unveiled-mount-dora-florida/5827701001/.

The House That Hats Built: https://www.stetsonmansion.com/john-b-stetson-biography; https://www.visitflorida.com/travel-ideas/articles/arts-history-stetson-museum-luxury-estate-florida/; https://www.deland.org/320/History-of-DeLand.

Pounding the Pavement: https://floridacitrushalloffame.com/inductees/hoyle-pounds/; https://www.orlandosentinel.com/news/os-xpm-2000-09-21-0009190376-story.html.

History in the Halls: https://historicedgewater.com/; https://downtownwg.com/locations/west-orange-trail/.

A Deep Dive in the Middle of Florida: None

Calling Quetzalcoatl: None

Once upon a Time in Maitland: https://enzian.org/about/; https://www.scottjosephorlando.com/news/78-scotts-news/191-chow-hound-report-enzians-eden-bar-opens.

Death in Altamonte Springs: https://metalgraveyardblog.wordpress.com/chuck-schulinder/; https://en.wikipedia.org/wiki/Death_metal; https://www.last.fm/music/Death/+wiki.

Rock Springs Revisited: None

Walt Disney on Ice: Biography — Is Walt Disney's Body Frozen? https://www.biography.com/news/walt-disney-frozen-after-death-myth; "The Further Adventures of Walt's Frozen Head," 2018, Benjamin Lancaster, Just A Head In A Jar.

A View from the Top: https://www.insider.com/inside-disneys-secret-cinderella-castle-suite-2016-11; https://www.wdwinfo.com/disney-world/magic-kingdom/cinderella-castle.htm.

X Marks the Spot: https://www.orlandosentinel.com/opinion/os-xpm-2013-11-21-os-ed-disney-property-anniversary-112113-20131120-story.html; https://www.wptv.com/news/state/the-history-behind-walt-disney-world; https://www.atlasobscura.com/places/disney-collection-orlando-public-library.

It Takes a Villages: https://247wallst.com/city/the-villages-fl-will-be-among-the-fastest-growing-cities-by-2060; https://www.insidethebubble.net/; https://toughnickel.com/real-estate/Advantages-and-Disadvantages-of-Living-in-The-Villages-Florida.

A Hidden Gem among the Bricks: www.florida.legoland.com; https://www.fox13news.com/news/the-history-of-cypress-gardens-floridas-first-theme-park/.

Ghoul's Night Out: None

On the Cutting Edge: https://www.atlasobscura.com/places/randall-knife-museum; https://www.randallknives.com/randall-history/.

Curious Goods: None

Deep Canyons in a Flat State: www.zipthecanyons.com; https://www.rvthereyettv.com/2022/01/fort-desoto-alternate-plans.html; https://www.tampabay.com/features/travel/florida/zip-line-novice-dares-ocalas-canyons/1225840/.

British Invasion: None

The Bridge to Nowhere: https://www.orlandosentinel.com/news/breaking-news/os-wekiva-river-bridge-to-nowhere-20150425-story.html.

Festive-Sounding Fortress: https://www.nbbd.com/godo/FortChristmas/; http://fchsinfo.com/cracker-christmas/; www.OrangeCountyParks.net.

Have Space Suit, Will Donate: None

Space to Roam: https://www.inforum.com/weather/weathertalk-we-launch-rockets-from-cape-canaveral-because-of-good-rocket-science; https://www.kennedyspacecenter-tickets.com/kennedy-space-center-nasa/.

I've a Feeling We're Not in Cape Canaveral Anymore: https://www.wizardofozflorida.com/

Digging Our History: https://en.wikipedia.org/wiki/Windover_Archeological_Site; https://www.thehistorycenter.org/windover/; https://www.usatoday.com/story/news/nation/2013/12/23/windover-bog/4146659/.

Keeping Watch on an Island: www. floridastateparks.org/hontoonisland; https://www.hmdb.org/m. asp?m=189124; https://www.sjrwmd. com/waterways/st-johns-river/.

A Spirited Discussion: https:// en.wikipedia.org/wiki/Cassadaga,_ Florida; https://www.thehistorycenter. org/cassadaga/.

Where the Surf Glows under the Full Moon: None

One for the Road: https://www. atlasobscura.com/places/last-resort; https://www.miaminewtimes.com/ news/does-the-ghost-of-aileen-wuornos-haunt-this-florida-dive-bar-13196021; https://www. nydailynews.com/news/national/ public-fascinated-serial-killer-aileen-wuornos-article-1.1236968.

The Ruins of NSB: None

The Path of Enlightenment: https://www. youtube.com/watch?v=QUr5brCHhbg; https://www.orlandosentinel.com/ politics/os-mims-buddhist-center-20170519-story.html; https://www. roadsideamerica.com/tip/46876.

Racing from the Beginning: https:// streamlinehotel.com/; https:// www.dailymail.co.uk/travel/ article-11803355/Inside-Florida-hotel-known-birthplace-NASCAR-haunt-Al-Capone.html; https://www. codb.us/365/History-of-City.

All That and a Bag of Chips: https:// www.orlandoweekly.com/food-drink/ in-its-16-years-stardust-video-and-coffee-has-become-a-vital-cultural-crossroads-for-orlando-2455552; https://www.orlandoweekly.com/ orlando/stardust-video-and-coffee/ Location?oid=2290117; https:// stardustvideoandcoffee.wordpress. com/info-2/.

Fiberglass Menagerie: https://www. roadsideamerica.com/tip/67704.

Monkey Business at the Springs: https://www.nationalgeographic. com/animals/article/florida-rhesus-monkeys-herpes-running-wild-invasive-species; https:// www.floridannature.com/ SilverSpringsFlorida.htm; https:// www.fox13news.com/news/its-raining-monkeys-florida-man-records-monkeys-jumping-from-trees-into-river-at-silver-springs-state-park.

Hidden in the Hammock: www. theblackhammock.com; https://www. orlandosentinel.com/travel/explore-florida/os-exfl-central-black-hammock-airboats-20160509-story.html.

Swirled Domination: https://www. sfgate.com/hawaii/article/ Disney-Dole-Whip-origin-not-Hawaii-17233525.php#:~:text=A%20 dairy%2Dfree%2C%20 fruit%2D,then%20Disneyland%20 Park%20in%201986; https://www. disneyfoodblog.com/dole-whip-at-disney-a-historical-timeline; https://www.atlasobscura.com/ foods/pineapple-dole-whip-disney; https://laist.com/news/food/the-history-of-dole-whip; https://www. wdw-magazine.com/disneys-beloved-dole-whip-is-coming-to-grocery-stores-near-you/#:~:text=While%20 you%20previously%20could%20 try,coming%20to%20grocery%20 stores%20soon.

A Ghost of a Chance: https://www. orlandosentinel.com/news/os-xpm-1990-08-05-9008030359-story. html; http://www.weirdus.com/states/ florida/unexplained_phenomena/ oviedo_lights/index.php.

Spook Hill in Lake Wales: www. visitcentralflorida.org/destinations/ spook-hill; https://www.nps.gov/ places/spook-hill.htm.

The Monsters at the End of This Book: https://www.facebook.com/ godmonsters.

RELIQUARY

JASON VOORHEES ALIVE!

MISSING

MISSING TEEN TAKEN BY FREDDY KRUEGER

CHEMICAL LEAK CAUSES OUTBREAK OF PUNK ROCK ZOMBIES

HAVE YOU SE

Cocktails and Screams

INDEX